Machine Embroidery with Style

dj BENNETT

Madrona Publishers   *Seattle*

TO *Ken,*
WHO MAKES IT ALL WORTHWHILE

Library of Congress Cataloging in Publication Data

Bennett, Dj, 1926-
  Machine embroidery with style.

  (Connecting threads)
  Bibliography: p.
  1. Embroidery, Machine. I. Title. II. Series.
TT772.B46   746.44'028   80-13914
ISBN 0-914842-45-5

Acknowledgments

My sincere thanks to Joy Clucas, who introduced me to machine embroidery; to Bev Rush for the generous sharing of her experience and enthusiasm; to my many students for questions that demanded answers; to my family for their enthusiastic support; and to the editorial staff of Madrona Publishers for connecting all the threads.

Black-and-white photo finishing by Robert E. Mattson, Jr.

All work shown in this book, all drawings, and all photographs except photo of dj Bennett are by the author.

Published by
Madrona Publishers, Inc.
2116 Western Avenue
Seattle, Washington 98121

Contents

PART TWO: Personal Ways to Use and Expand Your Skills

1. *Needle drawing: straight and satin stitch.*

Machine embroidery is the only new embroidery technique in centuries. It began in the Singer workrooms in New York City in the 1880s. An early Singer publication shows examples of machine embroidery with directions for cutwork and satin stitching that imitated the finest hand embroidery. To satin stitch, the book suggests drawing two lines about half an inch apart on the fabric, then moving the fabric (in a hoop) back and forth under the stationary needle while coordinating the horizontal motion with the up-and-down strokes of the needle, emulating on a treadle machine the swing (zigzag) needle of forty years later. I think it is safe to say that not many embroiderers perfected this demanding skill. Because this technique was originally intended to imitate hand embroidery so closely, only the few who were very technically skilled could realize any satisfaction from it, and it died a natural death soon after—at least so far as the United States was concerned.

In England, a few dedicated artists such as Dorothy Benson, in Singer's London workrooms, and Rebecca Crompton, who worked with her at the Bromley School of Art, inspired enthusiasm and experimentation during the 1920s and 30s. The invention of the swing-needle sewing machine in the 1950s, coupled with a gradual awakening of interest in all creative fiber techniques, led to the realization that machine embroidery had potential as an art form in its own right, rather than as a mechanized version of hand embroidery.

Embroiderers will recognize the similarities and

2. Machine embroidery could be done on machines such as this nineteenth-century treadle Singer—but it was only for the most determined and patient women. Photograph courtesy of the Singer Company, Stamford, Connecticut.

differences between hand and machine embroidery, and creative stitchers will take advantage of both techniques. Like the hand-held needle, the machine is an extension of the hand, a distinct and versatile tool when used by the creative embroiderer. In hand embroidery, the needle moves in and out in all directions across the surface of a stationary fabric. In machine embroidery, the fabric is moved in all directions under a fixed, stabbing needle. Hand embroidery can be slow and time-consuming; machine embroidery is fast. The stem stitch, running stitch, and back stitch are all used to achieve distinctive linear effects in hand embroidery, but none of these can equal the sensitive mobility of the machined line (which I'm sure Picasso would have loved; it would have suited his splendid feeling for the linear). Machine embroidery is generally more durable than hand embroidery, making it ideal for decorating clothing, table linens, and anything else that requires repeated laundering. The closely worked machined satin stitch lies flat on the surface of the fabric and is less subject to snagging and pulling than the traditional hand-worked satin stitch done in crewel wools. And there are equally important but less obvious characteristics of machine embroidery that must be explored through doing; hence this working primer presents a step-by-step progression of learning skills.

The book is divided into seven lessons plus three sections of ideas, suggestions, and diagrams for the reader to use as take-off points for individualized projects once the basic skills have been mastered. Lesson 2 involves a discussion of color and compositon which, although very necessary for any serious study of embroidery, might not be of immediate importance to all stitchers. Study this section when the need arises, or use it in its present sequence as a preliminary to a more comprehensive investigation of machine embroidery.

Browse through the last three sections first and look at the pictures, then begin the lessons. It is important that you follow them in succession because each builds upon the previous one. Each lesson (with the exception of Lesson 2) introduces a different basic technique explored through the study of a simple, familiar shape: the apple. After the fashion of nineteenth-century primers, we will do exercises, making a small individual sample to illustrate each technique. The final lesson deals with joining these samples into one large finished wall hanging. The end result will be not only a piece of well-designed machine embroidery but a functional, working sampler of basic techniques in the tradition of the seventeenth-century "examplars" that were passed from mother to daughter, added to and developed, in lieu of formal textbooks on embroidery. You are creating your own twentieth-century textbook which will be the expression of a new and exciting skill for you, the machine embroiderer.

3. Picasso would have loved machine embroidery for its sensitive mobility of line.

Part One

A PRIMER OF MACHINE EMBROIDERY

Lesson 1: How to Begin

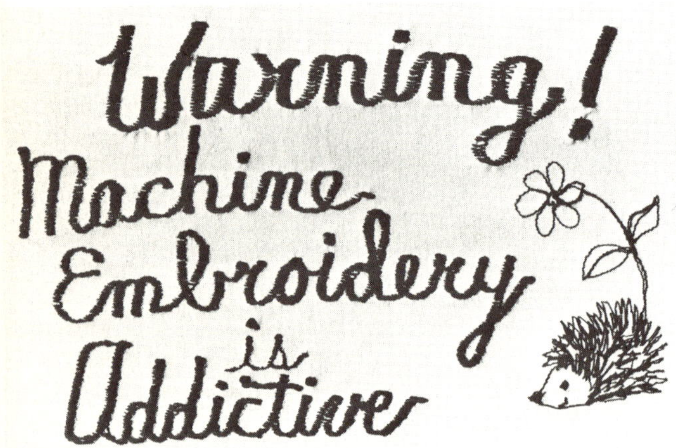

CARE OF YOUR MACHINE

Machine embroidery makes more rigorous demands upon your machine than ordinary dressmaking does, and it is important that you care for the machine properly. First of all, read the manual that came with your machine. Know the basic parts, where the oil points are, and how to adjust tensions. In other words, get to know your machine better. Clean lint and fuzz from the teeth (under the sole plate) each time you embroider. This prevents a sluggish machine and broken needles. Oil the bobbin where the bobbin case fits into its metal socket each time you embroider (one tiny drop of oil will suffice). You'll hear the difference as it purrs. Oil all other oil points every twelve to fourteen hours of embroidery—regardless of what your manual says about oiling. Metal moving on metal must be lubricated. But use the oil sparingly, use only regular sewing-machine oil, and learn to listen to the sound of your machine. You'll be able to hear when it's happy.

GENERAL INSTRUCTIONS

Machine embroidery is worked by moving fabric under a needle rather than by moving a hand-held needle in and out across the fabric. The fabric is usually framed in an embroidery hoop. Any kind of fabric can be used: simple muslin and calico, nets and sheers, velvets and corduroys, and anything in between. Care must be taken, however, with fabrics that are stretchy and unstable, such as knits. These must be stabilized by framing them up with a piece of organdy or muslin on the back in order to reduce their tendency to move in the frame. Some velvets and deep-pile fabrics will retain the marks of the hoop and should not be used by a beginner unless the hoop marks occur outside the limits of the design.

It is of extreme importance that the fabric be stretched drum-head tight in a wooden embroidery hoop with a screw adjustment. Wrap the inner circle of the hoop with twill tape or something comparable for better contact with the fabric. Use the hoop in what would normally be an upside-down position so that the fabric lies flat and right side up on the surface of the machine. Place the fabric in the hoop flat on a table, grasp the *edges* of the fabric with both hands, and *push* toward the *center* of the hoop, tightening as much as possible, all the way around the circle. Tighten the screw and push the fabric again. Continue to do this until the fabric is as tight as you can get it. If the fabric is not framed properly it will vibrate and bounce under the needle, causing annoying thread breakage.

Any kind of thread that will go through a sewing-machine needle may be used in machine embroidery; heavier threads may be used in the bobbin. Some Singers insist on having the same type of thread (cotton, polyester, or cotton-polyester blend) top and bottom, so learn the whims of your particular machine, but most machines don't mind a bit using different threads top and bottom. Use a large-size needle—90 to 100 (14 to 16)—depending upon your brand of machine. And have several extra needles on hand—you'll inevitably break some.

Most machine embroidery is done with the presser foot removed and the teeth either depressed or covered, depending upon your machine. Consult your manual for specific instructions concerning this. If your machine is quite old you may not be able to do either. In that case, raise the sole plate just enough to clear the teeth by using small

4. *Grasp the near edges of the fabric and push the material in your hands toward the center of the circle. Work all the way around the hoop in this fashion, tighten the hoop screw, and repeat the process until the fabric is drum-head taut.*

washers or circles of cardboard with the screws. (It's a chore to put the washers on and off repeatedly. My first machine presented this problem and I simply ignored the teeth and went ahead as if they weren't there. The only difficulty was that certain fabrics, particularly nets and sheers, had a tendency to catch and snag on the teeth.) Depressing the teeth allows you to freely move the embroidery hoop under the needle in all directions. Run the machine at a fairly fast speed. This does not mean that the hoop has to be moved that fast. It's a little like patting your tummy and rubbing your head—the needle goes fast but the hoop and fabric can move at any speed. If the machine runs too slowly there is danger of the needle catching in the fabric, being pulled against the sole plate, and breaking. So keep up the machine speed.

AN IMPORTANT WORD OF CAUTION

The trouble that beginners most frequently experience in machine embroidery is thread clogging the bobbin. Nine times out of ten this happens because the presser foot is up. It is very easy to forget to lower the presser-foot bar, especially when the foot has been removed. From the beginning, train yourself always to lower the presser-foot bar before starting to stitch. If your machine sputters and spits and coughs and you get all kinds of interesting loopy textures on the back of your fabric, you've forgotten to lower that bar. Cheer up; everyone has done it!

SUPPLY LIST

The following are what you'll need in order to do the lessons and will want to have on hand later on.

> A sewing machine with a swing needle (for zigzag stitching), plus the accessory feet provided with the machine. In addition to the standard feet for dressmaking, recommended feet are
>
> > A quilting or darning foot (either of which has some form of spring shank to allow

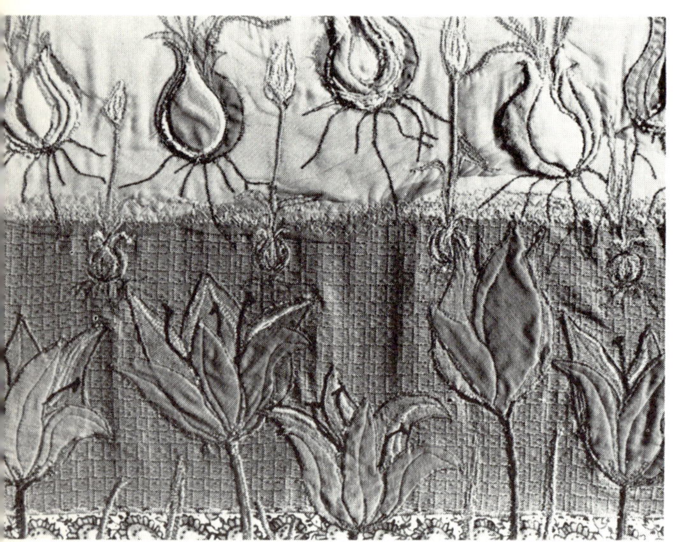

5. *Spring detail of the Four Seasons Panel: bulbs and tulips of appliquéd sheers and velvets on plain and printed fabrics. Embroidery is worked in straight and satin stitches.*

the fabric to move freely);
An embroidery foot (with a wide groove on the bottom to prevent heavy build-up of threads underneath the foot).

The owner's manual. Depending on age and model, machines vary in small details (for example, stitch width-and-length scales, tension-change mechanism, teeth control), so learn to refer to your owner's manual when any mechanical question arises.

An apple or two.

Sewing-machine thread: cotton, cotton-polyester blend, polyester, or rayon, in colors found in the apples. (Machine embroidery uses lots of thread, so have plenty on hand.)

Heavier thread: No. 3 and No. 5 perle cotton, crochet cotton, Bella Donna, one-ply Persian wool, knitting worsted, and rug yarn for starters.

Assorted fabrics color-related to the thread: cotton, cotton-synthetic blends (no knits), nets, sheers, old nylon hose. These should be no smaller than a 12-inch square, but no one kind need exceed half a yard. Variety is desirable, so include different textures, some patterned, some plain. Choose one color to be dominant.

Dacron polyfill or batting for padding (a handful or two).

A thin wooden* embroidery hoop with a screw-type adjustment, 8 or 10 inches in diameter. Be sure the hoop is thin enough to slip under a sewing-machine presser-foot shank when the foot is removed. (Some older machines have extra-long

6. *Machine embroidery is especially suitable for the spikes of a hedgehog or fur of a raccoon. This hedgehog from the Four Seasons Caftan has stiff grey-and-white spikes made from two colors of thread through one needle. Flowers and stems are satin stitched.*

---

*The fabric must be extremely tight in the hoop, and only wooden hoops will hold it properly. Metal ones have a spring adjustment that gives, and plastic hoops are too flexible. Later you will find an 8- or 10-inch circle of fabric is not the right size to accommodate your design or idea, and you will find it advantageous to have a number of hoops of various sizes.

7. *Summer/autumn detail of the Four Seasons Panel: berry bushes on heavily textured drapery fabric in a combination of straight, satin, and cable stitches plus blobs, couching, and appliqué. Applied materials at the bottom are nylon hose, net, and plastic mesh from a vegetable bag.*

presser-foot shanks that prevent the hoop from sliding under. In this case tilt the hoop on edge to ease it under the shank.) Wind the inside ring of the hoop with twill tape for better contact with the fabric.

Two and a half yards of checked gingham, 1-inch check pattern, color-coordinated to threads.

One yard of unbleached muslin.

Large machine needles (90 to 100 or the equivalent).

Double needle if available for your machine.

Chalk for drawing designs on fabric.

Pins.

Plastic wrap or Stitch Witchery (optional).

Occasionally an exercise or project will involve an attachment or piece of equipment that your machine doesn't have. In such a case just move on to the next paragraph. The only firm requirement for machine embroidery is the swing needle for zigzag stitching.

GETTING STARTED FOR FREE MACHINING

Frame up a test piece of unbleached muslin. Tighten the fabric, tighten the screw, tighten the fabric again. Tap it—it should sound tight and firm. Now, step by step, check off the following:

Presser foot removed.

Machine threaded top and bottom (always have the presser-foot bar *up* when threading to assure proper tension).

Tension set at normal, top and bottom.

Teeth depressed or covered.

Stitch width adjusted for straight stitching.

Stitch length: of no consequence if teeth are depressed.

Your machine is now ready for free machining with a

straight stitch. This is the setting to use when future lessons require free machining.

Now place the fabric in the hoop under the needle and lower the presser-foot bar. Dip the needle to bring up the bottom thread and take your first stitch in this same hole to lock the threads in place.

EXERCISE 1. Write your name. This is a familiar motion. Run the machine quite fast, but move the fabric at a comfortable speed, forming the letters of your name. Write just as you would on paper, but move your "paper" rather than the "pen." *Keep your fingers close to the needle* and guide the movement with your thumbs and little fingers. (Keeping your fingers close to the needle will give you much better control and will prevent the fabric from vibrating, reducing the danger of thread breakage. Don't worry about your fingers—you'll quickly learn how to do this and you'll develop confidence rapidly.) Notice how you can move the fabric in the hoop freely in *all* directions—up and down, sideways, in circles—without any difficulty.

Don't worry if your name isn't quite legible the first few times (or even if you've misspelled it!). Think how long it took in kindergarten.

Machined threads are anchored by stitching up and down several times in one place. To move from one stitched area to another, first anchor your stitching, then raise the presser-foot bar, move your hoop to the next area, and continue to stitch. The intervening threads may be clipped later.

Cover the entire fabric area with your name. See what patterns you can create with the motion. Letters of the alphabet can be an interesting design unit, so relax your shoulders and take advantage of the lovely linear quality of the machined lines. Please don't destroy this first little sample. Keep each one of your efforts—you'll be surprised how nicely they will work into your final piece. Besides, they will record your progress!

EXERCISE 2. Try another sample of your name using the zigzag stitch. (Be aware that the terms *zigzag* and *swing* are generally interchangeable. When I indicate the number at

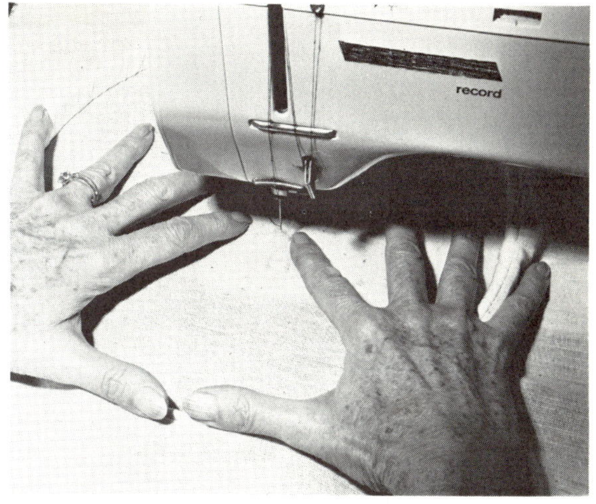

8. *Keeping your index fingers close to the needle, move the frame with your thumbs and little fingers.*

9. *From top to bottom, these names were free machined with straight stitch, with the zigzag set at 2½, and with the zigzag set at 4.*

which to set the swing, that tells you how wide the stitch will be.) In this case, start with a medium zigzag (2 on a scale of 4), then try 3 and 4. Notice the variation of line that occurs as you move the fabric from right to left. This variation is one of the main characteristics of machining and is not attainable in any other type of embroidery, so learn to take advantage of it. By now you have recognized that this free-machine setting can be used for a wider line by adjusting the stitch-width control. Later you'll see how this same setting can be used not only for lines but for filling areas. Save your samples from this exercise.

10. Hedgehogs and strawberries: needle drawing using both straight and satin stitches.

Lesson 2: Embroidery Tools — Color and Related Elements of Composition

Most of us—embroiderers or any other kind of craftsman—know that work, attractive materials, and technical skill do not necessarily add up to a beautiful finished product. In many crafts, and embroidery especially, some knowledge of the elements of composition makes a great difference in the final result.

Some of you will want to give this information immediate and serious study; others will simply want to bypass it and come back later. Either way, read the two exercises because they contain useful information.

Design is the arranging of elements of a composition, and no matter how elementary or sophisticated your embroidery, composition plays an important part in it. A good composition holds together, is interesting to look at, and has a good relationship between positive and negative areas. (The positive areas are the stitched ones; the negative areas are the unstitched.)

In embroidery there are six elements of composition: color, line, texture, area, value, and volume. Knowledge of how to best use these six comes partly from sharpening one's awareness of these elements in daily surroundings. But first you have to know what you're looking for, so I'll be

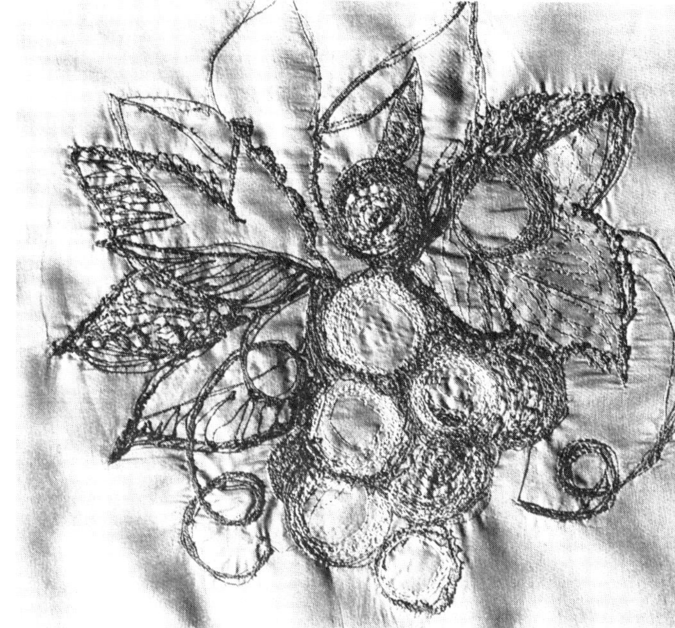

11. *A grape and leaf design in straight stitch on silk.*

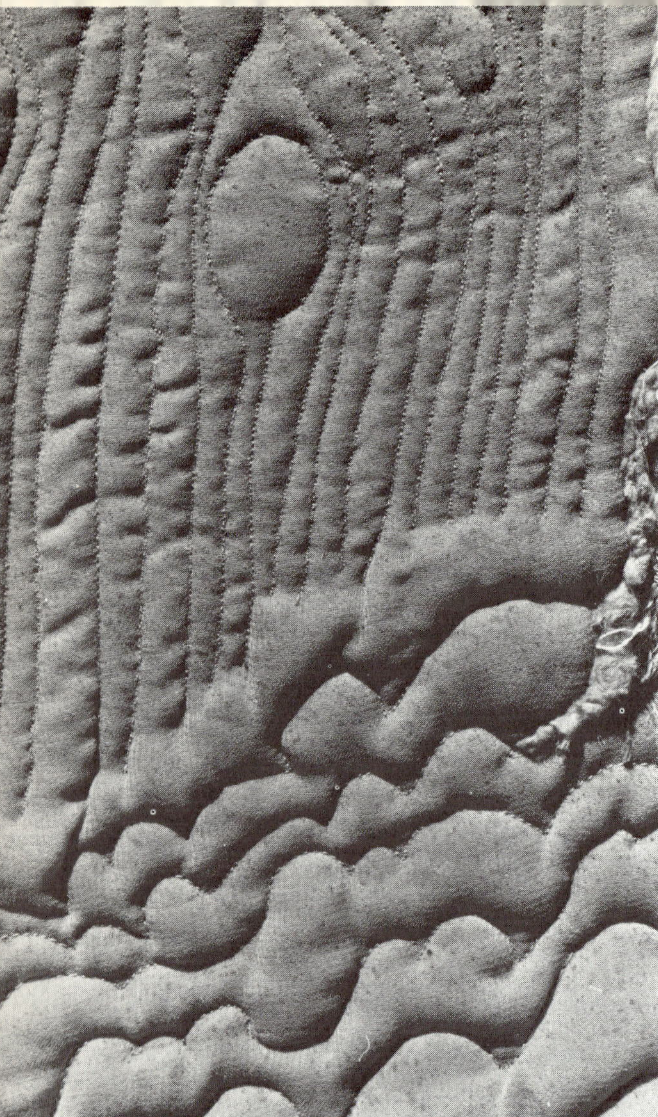

12. *Quilting depends upon the play of light on contoured surfaces for its impact. A simple monochromatic scheme shows this to good advantage.*

including information about these six at the same time I'm helping you develop your machine-embroidery skills.

CHARACTERISTICS OF COLOR

Color is one of the most appealing elements of composition and it certainly is one of the most personal. The range of colors available in sewing threads alone is enough to make the heart sing. For that reason I feel it is more important that you enjoy the colors you use in your work than to worry about rules for the use of color.

But the time may come when you find that, although you have used quantities of your favorite colors, somehow, when all together, they simply don't create the beautiful effect you had hoped for. A deep, rich brown suddenly looks much too green; that splendid area of orange fights violently with the equally splendid purple. At this point some basic knowledge of color principles might help solve your problem.

It is difficult to speak of any kind of color without referring to the color wheel, that circular rainbow composed of the primary, secondary, and tertiary colors. By way of review, a primary color is that pure hue from which other colors may be mixed; it is basic and cannot be mixed from other colors. The primaries are red, yellow, and blue. Secondary colors result from mixing primaries. Red and yellow make orange, yellow and blue make green, red and blue make violet. Tertiary colors, such as russet, citron, and olive, result from the mixture of a primary and a secondary and create some of the lovely subtle off-tones so dear to the hearts of embroiderers.

A twelve-color wheel (which can be purchased at art-supply stores) consists of the three primary colors, three secondary colors, and six tertiary colors, each midway between a primary and a secondary color.

Hue is color in its purest form—red, green, violet, orange. A tint is a lighter value of a hue (pink is a tint of red); a shade is a darker value of a hue (burgundy is a shade of red).

Intensity (saturation) indicates the degree or amount of pure hue involved.

Colors have temperature; there are warm colors—yellow, red orange, yellow green—and cool colors—blue, sea green, and lavender blue. Warm colors tend to excite and stimulate; cool colors tend to soothe and relax. Warm colors advance from a background; cool colors recede. Soft, soothing sea greens and quiet blues would probably work best for a wall hanging in a dentist's office, while vibrant yellows and reds would be more appropriate for cushions in a ski lodge.

Color Schemes

There are several basic color schemes from which the embroiderer might choose. The first is *monochromatic*, a scheme that uses only one hue and all the various tints and shades related to that hue. It is this color scheme, above all others, that really shows off the textural qualities of stitches, particularly when whites and off-whites are used. This is the favorite color scheme of those who are primarily interested in stitches, or in quilting, which depends upon the play of light upon contoured surfaces for its interest.

A *complementary* color scheme uses hues directly opposite each other on the color wheel (and, of course, their corresponding tints and shades). This can be a very dramatic scheme, particularly if one hue predominates (such as green with its tints and shades, then a carefully planned, selectively used splash of red for contrast). Most of your samples will fall into this scheme, with the addition of black and white, of course. The more equal the amounts of the two hues used, the more static and uninteresting the result.

A *split complementary* color scheme involves a hue plus two colors, one on either side of the hue's direct complement (for example, a bottle green with an orange mauve and a violet mauve). This can be a bit more difficult to handle, but it is often very satisfying because it involves some of the more subtle, less frequently used tones. Later, you'll find that layers of colored net and sheers will help in the mixing of tones.

13. A rich monochromatic scheme achieved through white hand embroidery, white machine embroidery, and applied pearls. With emphasis on texture, values, and variety of stitches, color becomes unimportant.

Perhaps the most vivid of all color schemes is the *analogous* or *adjacent* color scheme, involving colors side by side on the color wheel. Technically this scheme should involve only one dominant primary, which limits it to any third of the twelve-color wheel. If a second primary assumes almost equal importance, you've gone too far around the wheel. Adjacent colors enrich and intensify each other, so the overall effect is one of vibrant, glowing richness, much like that of stained glass.

Then there are the *neutral* or noncolor schemes, those based on black, white, and grey. These should be considered separately since black and white do not appear on the color wheel. They are important in that they provide the embroiderer with elements of dramatic impact as well as perfect foils against which to successfully work brilliant colors.

Neutrals that contain only black and/or white are *achromatic* (noncolor) neutrals. There are also *chromatic* (colored) neutrals; these are the neutrals that usually work best with other colors. A slightly greenish white is more compatible with a predominately green composition than a pure white would be—pure, cold white could deaden an otherwise rich color scheme. The same is true of black. A black to which a touch of red has been added works better with warm hues than would a pure, achromatic black. And then there is my friend who tried her best through reading, study, and inquiry to discover what scheme included red, white, and blue. The only definitive answer seemed to be patriotic!

EFFECTS OF VARIOUS COMBINATIONS

The above is the basic vocabulary of colors, but it is of little value to the embroiderer unless used meaningfully with threads and fabric. A few observations might be helpful here. As already mentioned, warm colors advance, cool colors recede; awareness of this can be used to give depth and perspective to a composition. A color scheme is

14. *Quilting (done with a double needle) and trapunto: another example of the effectiveness of a one-color scheme.*

more effective if it is predominately warm or cool; equal amounts of both tend to dull the entire scheme. On the other hand, equal amounts of complements of equal intensity (for example, equal amounts of red and green) will result in vibration, which can be used effectively, but often causes a distracting or disturbing effect. A dark spot of color looks larger on a light ground than on a dark one; conversely, a light spot looks larger on a dark ground. Careful use of this fact can add impact to your work. Adjacent colors appear more vivid when they are used next to each other. Large areas of a color appear lighter than one small spot of the same color.

Colors, like people, are affected by their surroundings. A warm color looks warmer against a cool ground; a cool color looks cooler against a warm ground. This is a result of what is known as the subtractive theory of color, in which like hues seem to cancel each other when used side by side. For instance, a violet thread on a blue fabric will appear much redder than the same thread on orange. The blue in the violet thread, along with the blue of the fabric, is canceled, leaving the visual image of a predominance of red in the violet thread. In the second case, the red in the violet thread, along with the red in the orange fabric, is canceled, creating the illusion of blue-violet thread. A brown thread on a violet fabric will take on a decided yellow cast, while the same brown on a green ground will look much redder. All of this seems a bit complex when it comes to using fabric and threads, but knowledge of this phenomenon can be of use to an embroiderer when certain colors simply don't behave the way they were expected to.

Certainly you should not sit down and carefully review these characteristics of color each time you embroider; let's hope your approach will be more spontaneous and joyful than that. But if, after choosing fabrics and threads, you have arranged and rearranged areas of color to get a general idea of how the color scheme will work, and something is wrong with the thing, then perhaps a review of the above will give some clue to a possible solution to your problem.

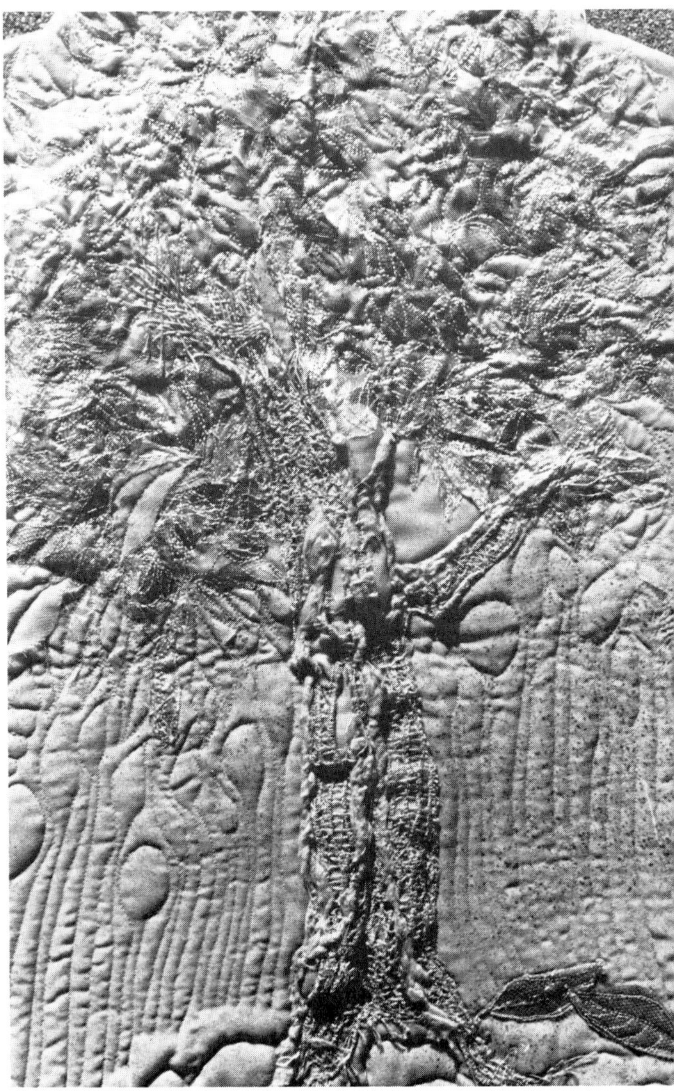

15. *Fantastic Tree: the trunk is needle lace, the ground fabric is spatter-painted free-machined chiffon, and the foliage is a collage of many fabrics and threads covered with plastic food wrap and stitched in straight stitch.*

HOW MANY COLORS IN AN APPLE?

Your various exercises or samples will be joined later in a patchwork composition, a sampler wall hanging with an apple as the source for your ideas. Look at an apple carefully. How many colors can you see in it? If you have a red apple chances are there will be a number of different tints and shades of red in it, as well as a touch of green. A bit of green enriches and intensifies red, making a dramatic and exciting complementary color scheme.

If you have a yellow apple there is probably a hint of yellow green in it as well as a rosy, yellow-orange blush. This is an analogous color scheme, composed of colors that lie side by side on the color wheel, and is a more subtle, often glowing scheme.

Now you probably can see many more colors than you did at first glance and realize how many different colors of thread you might need for your project. Is there a stem or a leaf? (More colors.) What colors of fabric do you think would harmonize with or accent the colors in your apple? Hold some fabric swatches up to it. How do they react to the threads you have chosen? Which combinations please you the most? These are the ones you will want to use for your composition.

Exercise 3. Make a collage using your apple as a model, with small samples of fabric and thread to illustrate all the colors you see in the apple (including tints, shades, and tones). Frame up one fabric as the ground, then arrange an interesting apple shape of fabric, threads, swatches, and ravelings on this ground fabric, using not only sewing-machine thread but rug yarn, knitting yarn, and other types of fiber. Add a bit of green to represent a leaf. Notice particularly where the dark and light areas are, and work them into your collage. When the composition pleases you, pin a piece of nylon hose over the entire area and free-machine stitch in straight stitching to enhance the design and fasten down the nylon. When you're done, trim off any surplus nylon. Notice what color scheme you have developed and what effect the nylon hose has had on the colors.

Exercise 4. Quilt a monochromatic composition. Frame up two pieces of lightweight, light-colored fabric with a thin layer of polyfill batting in between. Choose a thread color to carry out the monochromatic scheme. Drop the teeth and, using the straight stitch, free machine a small apple in the middle of your fabric. Stitch another, slightly larger apple, around this center one. Continue developing this apple outside an apple until the entire area is quilted, ending with an apple approximately the size of your hoop. In quilting, it is usually best to begin near the center of your composition and work in all directions toward the edges. Notice the pattern of lines you've created, as well as the interesting raised areas. Notice too how the pattern changes with the direction and intensity of the light source. Keep these samples for future reference.

ADVANCED COLOR/VALUE PROJECT

The following project is an advanced problem relating to colors and values and will require more technical skill than exercises 3 and 4. I suggest this one be done after finishing Lesson 7.

Make a machine-embroiderer's color wheel. On a piece of fabric of neutral color draw with a compass five concentric circles (wheels), each at least one inch from the next. To stitch your color wheel, you'll be using a hoop, free-machine

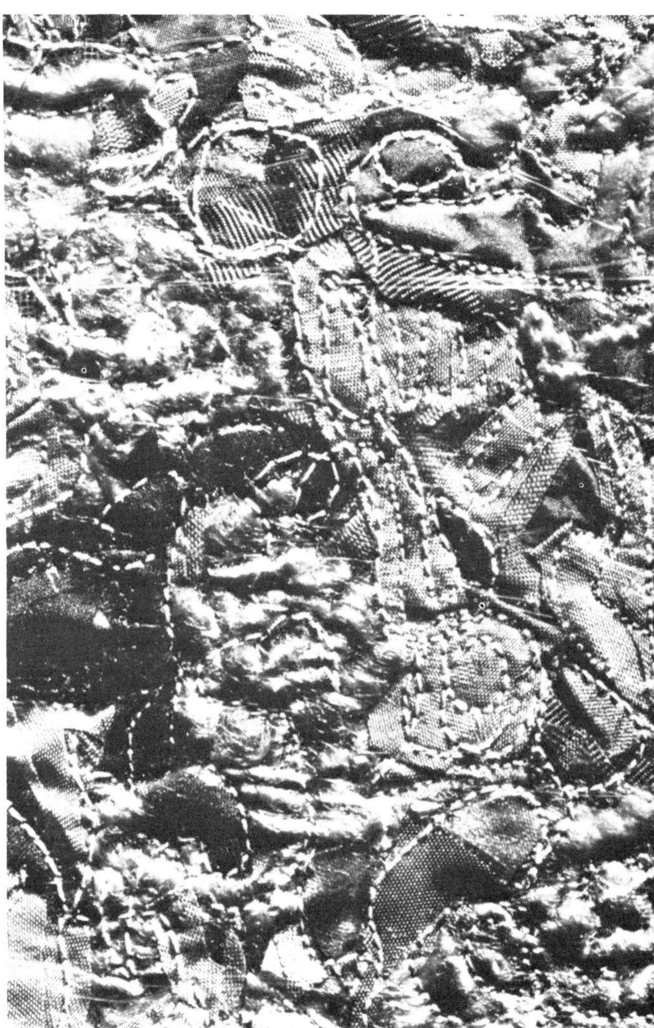

16. A multicolored collage of bits of fabric and thread held together by a layer of plastic food wrap, then stitched. Several layers of materials create a quilted effect.

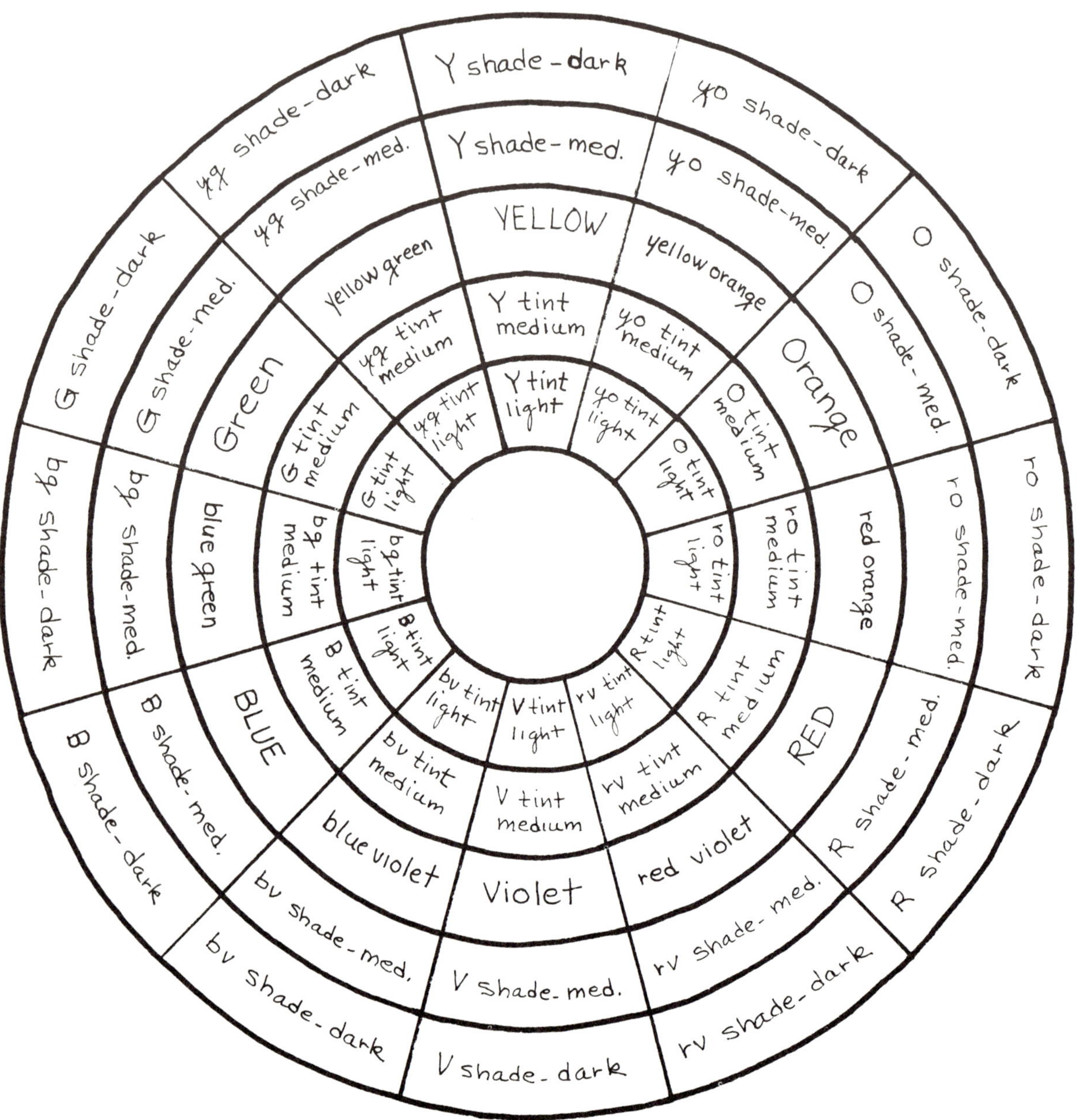

17. *A five-value color wheel shows twelve hues (ring three), two shades (the outer rings) and two tints (the inner rings). Primary colors are indicated by upper-case letters.*

settings, and, for best effect, all the machine techniques you've learned. Divide the wheels into twelve equal sections and embroider the central (third) wheel in the basic hues—three primaries, three secondaries, and six tertiaries. (Consult a professional color wheel for proper positions of hues if necessary.) Use a variety of embroidery techniques. Stitch wheel two (just outside the central one) in darker shades of each hue, and the outside wheel in still darker shades of each hue. Stitch the fourth wheel, just inside the basic one, in tints a bit lighter than each hue, and the innermost wheel, the fifth, in tints still lighter. Choose your hues, tints, and shades carefully, and you will have at hand not only a delightful circular rainbow and an invaluable working color wheel but, in your head, a decidedly more acute color perception.

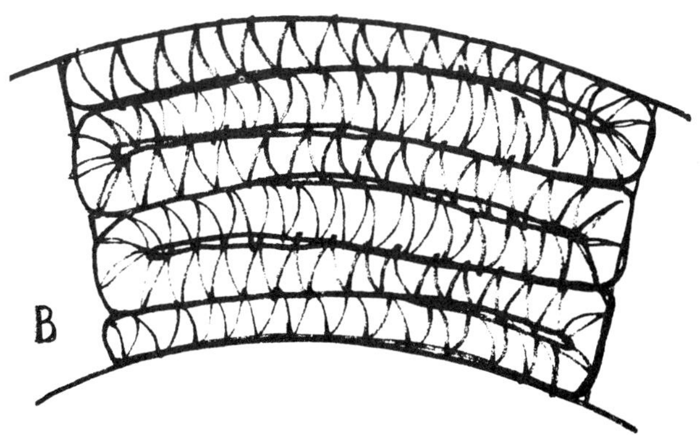

18. Details of preceding figure. A. Concentric lines of straight stitching form patterns of orange thread on red fabric, creating the effect of red orange. B. Heavy yellow rug yarn is couched with widely spaced green zigzag, creating the effect of an area filled with yellow green. In both cases positive and negative areas are blended to mix colors for the machine-stitched color wheel.

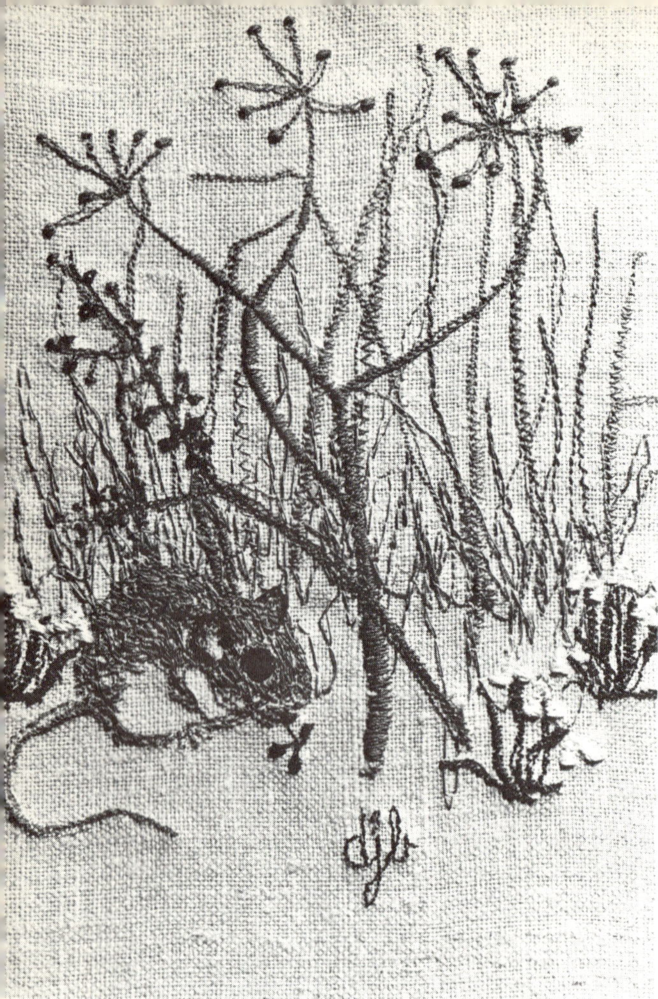

19. *The linear quality of free machining is ideal for expressing the delicate pattern of Queen Anne's lace, seed pods, and weeds.*

Lesson 3: Lines and Variations

USING LINE

Line is a way to connect two points and is an important element of composition. It expresses motion and direction, defines area, and leads the viewer from one place to another within a composition. Used properly, it can make the eye follow exactly where you want it to go—round and round within the area prescribed, rather than shooting off to the side and losing interest. One of the chief characteristics of machine embroidery is that it expresses line beautifully in a way that no other form of embroidery can.

You have already learned that you can move your fabric in all directions under the moving needle to create variations of line that add interest and variety to your stitchery. Let's examine these variations of line more closely by looking at one of your apples.

EXERCISE 5. Study the general shape of the apple. Is it round? Or oval? Or crooked? Is it flat at any spot? How much wider is it than high? Or is it higher than it is wide? Does it lean to one side or the other? Where does the stem come out in relation to the top? These are all questions that are related to composition and will make you look at that apple with special awareness.

After you have really studied your apple, frame up another piece of fabric and draw the apple with your needle. Don't draw it first with a pencil or chalk; you'd find it too difficult to follow your lines. Simply write an apple shape on the fabric the way you did your name. Try to exaggerate the characteristics that make this definitely your particular apple. Do several more of different sizes. Relax as you do it. Good! You probably surprised yourself. Keep this sample for future reference.

EXERCISE 6. Cut one of your apples in half from stem end to flower end. Notice the linear patterns of the stem, core, and seed areas. Notice how the lines flow from one to another. Study the overall shape of the half-apple. Frame up another piece of fabric, this time using a different color, and, with a straight stitch, stitch the cut half of the apple, concentrating on the linear patterns of the core.

EXERCISE 7. Try a variety of little shapes to indicate the core and seeds. Try some on different settings of stitch width for more line variation.

EXERCISE 8. Cut one of the halves in half lengthwise. Notice how the linear patterns change. Stitch a line sampler expressing this design.

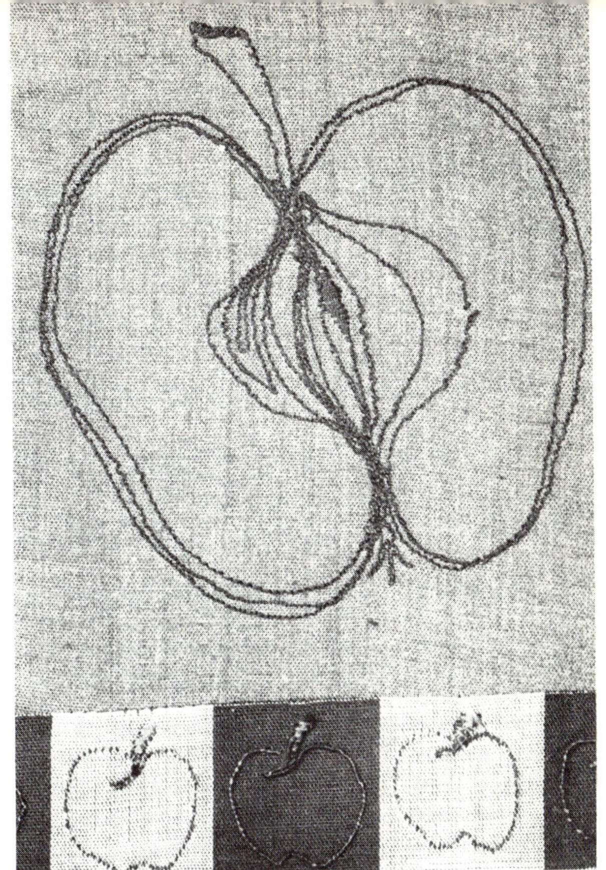

20. *There are many design possibilities in an apple. Here the mobile, free-stitched line suggests the shape of a halved apple, the pattern of its core, the concentration of its seeds, and—on the checks—a repetition of a whole apple.*

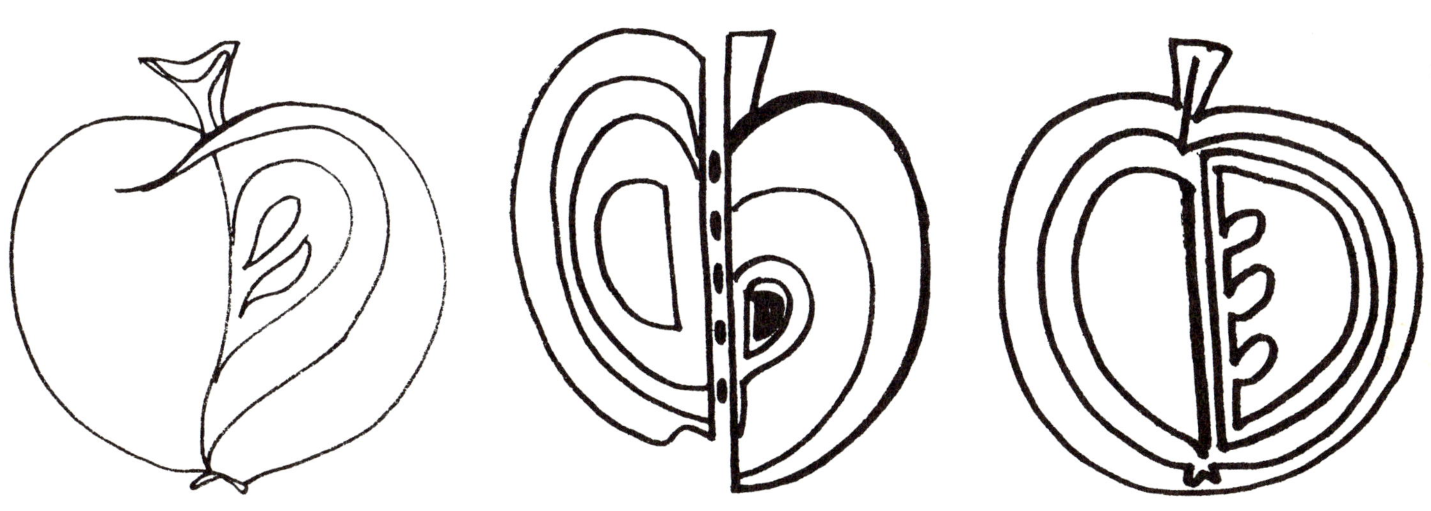

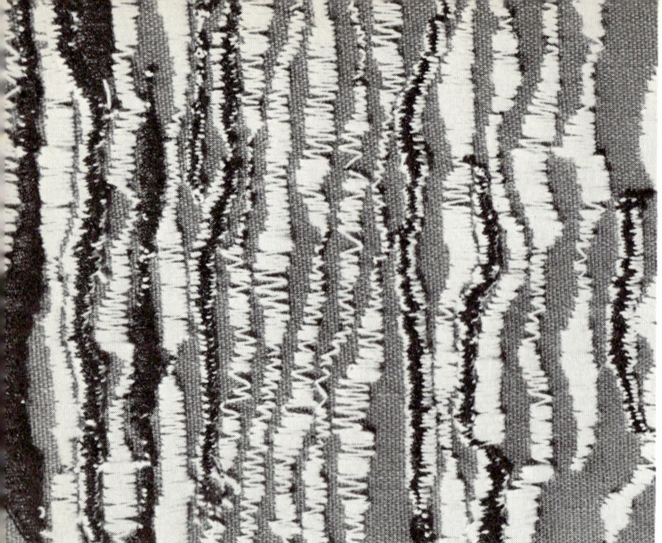

21. *Variation of line resulting from manual adjustment of the zigzag width while the machine is running. The fabric between the lines (negative space) is as important to the design as the stitching itself (positive space).*

22. *Grid lines showing variation of stitch lengths and widths.*

EXERCISE 9. Try another view of the quarter-apple with the zigzag set at 2. The variation of line will add a new dimension and interest to your design.

EXERCISE 10. Create a pattern of the letters A P P L E, spacing them in such a way that the negative areas (unstitched) form just as interesting a design as the positive areas (the stitched ones). Study your results carefully. An important aspect of good composition is a pleasing relationship between the positive and negative areas. Save all these samples.

VARIATIONS

There are two ways of varying a line in machine embroidery. You have made a start in both methods. The first is by manual adjustment—moving the knob or lever that regulates needle swing. By changing the width of the swing of the needle as you stitch, you can vary your line from practically no width to 3/8 inch. The other method involves changing the relationship between the swing of the needle and the motion of the fabric.

The manual-adjustment method takes practice; as you progress you'll learn to support and guide the hoop with one hand and control the adjustment knob with the other. It can be done, more easily than you might think, all while the machine is running. Give it a try (being sure your fabric is tightly framed).

EXERCISE 11. Make a grid. Grids are an interesting and simple way to create pleasing positive and negative areas. Manually changing the width of your zigzag as you stitch, create a grid of vertical and horizontal lines that cross each other to form negative areas of various sizes and shapes. Make the negative areas large enough to accommodate embroidery. In a few carefully selected areas formed by the grid, embroider different apple motifs—the whole apple, half-apple, seeds, cores, leaves.

Changing the relationship between the movement of the fabric and the swing of the needle will also result in line variation. Set your zigzag at 4 (the widest swing). Move your fabric from right to left, *with* the swing of the needle. What kind of line do you get? A relatively fine line, of course. Move the fabric from bottom to top, at *right angles* to the swing of the needle. Now the line is at its fullest width. With the setting still at 4, move the fabric from bottom to top in a gently waving line. Notice the nuances of linear change, a subtle variation that can be used to very good advantage in machine embroidery, and all without manual adjustment.

Notice, too, that the concentration of stitches changes the nature of the line. Moving the fabric quickly under the needle produces a light, jagged line. Moving the fabric more slowly results in a heavier, more solidly packed line. And when this line takes on added width, it becomes a satin stitch (Lesson 6). At this point line becomes area because it is filling in space. Practice these variations until you can predict what the line will do.

Exercise 12. Make leaves using both methods of linear variation. Follow the line in figure 24A, causing the line to vary as your fabric moves. Result: a graceful, elongated leaf shape. Try a leaf using the manual adjustment. This time follow the motion of figure 24B, manually changing the width of the zigzag swing. In leaf A, a freely stitched vein may be added; in B, the tiny unstitched channel between the two rows of stitching forms a natural vein. Embroider a leaf or two on one of your sampler apples.

LINE-SKILL PROJECTS

Once you have gained confidence in your ability to make lines, try the following more advanced projects:

A. Study the delicate linear patterns of Queen Anne's lace, milkweed, ferns, dried weeds. Interpret them in machine embroidery emphasizing the overall pattern of stitch concentration.

B. Using layers of overlapping net (greens, blues, blacks, reds), create the illusion of undersea light and shadow. Experiment with different thicknesses, directions of pattern, and color combinations to give the half-light, half-

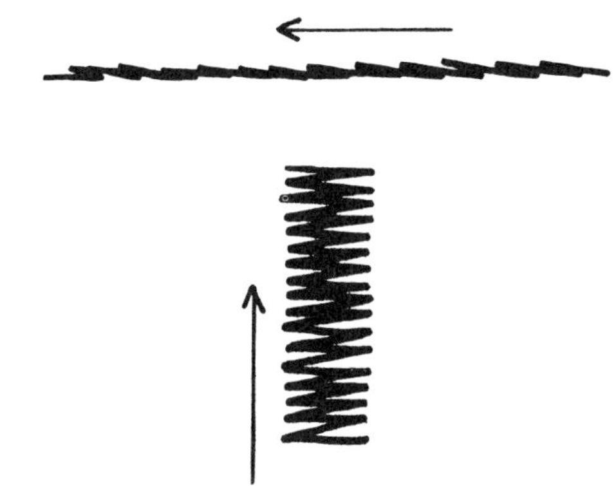

23. *Arrows indicate the direction in which the fabric is moved. Top: fabric moved from right to left (with the swing of the needle); bottom: fabric moved from bottom to top (at right angles to the swing of the needle).*

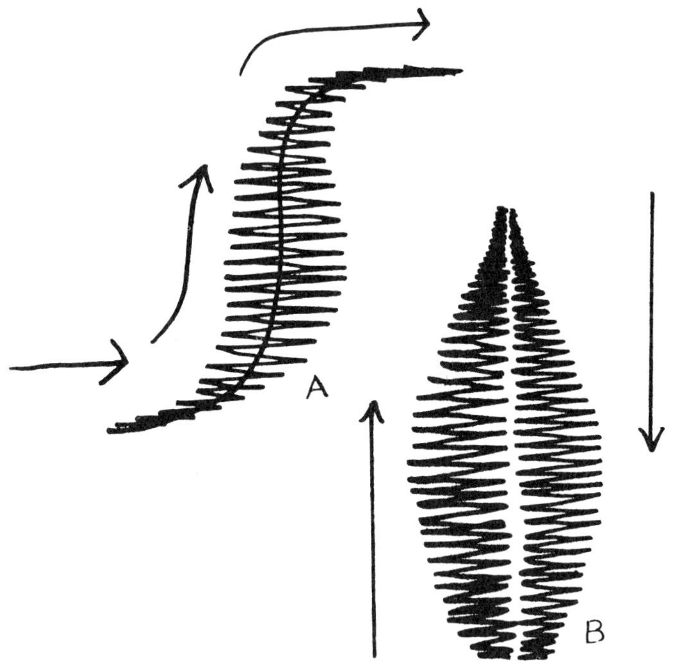

24. *Arrows indicate the path of the needle. A. The stitch-width setting remains on 4. B. The stitch width is manually adjusted from 1 to 4 to ½ (for the tip of the leaf).*

25. *Simple line stitching of autumn weeds.*

26. *Linear interpretation of foliage overlaid with net to create an illusion of depth, mist, and distance.*

deep illusion of water flowing over plants, shells, and stones. Let your imagination have full play here. Machine stitch over the net linear interpretations of coral, undersea plants, and the flow of currents over the bottom of the sea.

Monogramming

Once you've acquired line skills, you've learned the basic skill for monogramming. To monogram, start by drawing your monogram in *single-line script* on typing paper. (Alphabet patterns are available in needlework stores and art-supply shops. Better still, design your own.) Monogram a terrycloth towel by framing up the towel with the monogrammed paper pinned in proper position in the hoop. Set the zigzag at 3 or 4 and free stitch through both paper and fabric following the line of the drawn monogram.* Space the stitches close together by moving the fabric slowly, forming a line of satin stitch. Move the hoop on a straight horizontal axis, allowing the swing of the needle to create a natural variation of line. Move in a continuous, uninterrupted motion. Pull the paper pattern away from the towel after stitching.

*Embroidery worked directly over a paper pattern from the front works well on textured fabrics such as terrycloth. But inevitably bits of paper will be stitched into the embroidery, and they are extremely difficult to remove. For less heavily textured fabrics I would recommend the following: frame the paper pattern *drawn in reverse* on the wrong side of the fabric, then free stitch the basic contours with a straight stitch to mark the design. Remove the fabric and the paper from the frame and pull away the paper pattern; frame up to embroider from the right side, and embroider over the stitched design. With this method, bits of paper pattern will not interfere with your finished embroidery.

27. Monogram design drawn in single-line script on typing paper.

28. Paper pattern positioned on a framed terrycloth hand towel. Stitching follows the direction of the arrows.

29. Finished monogram, paper pattern removed.

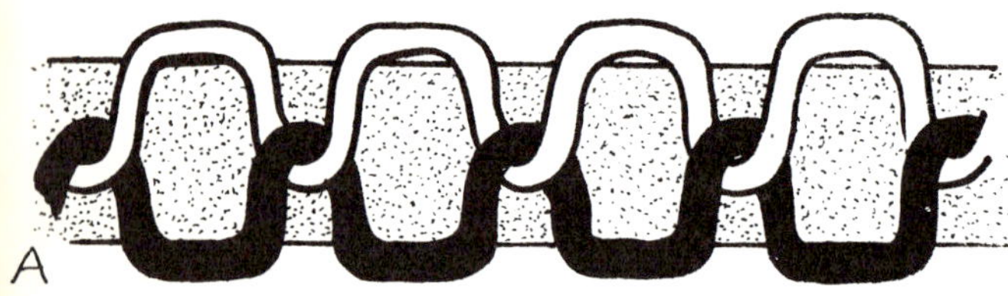

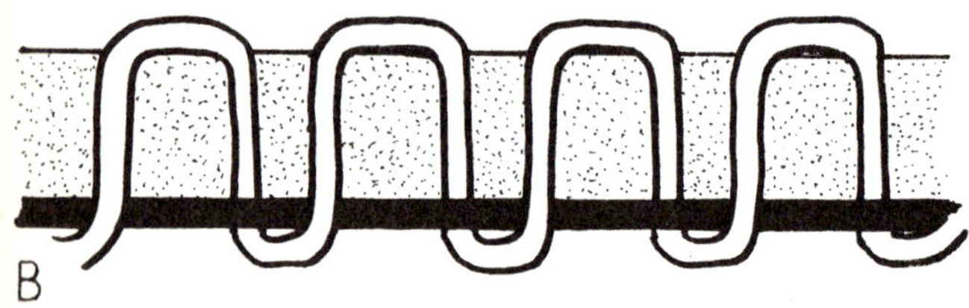

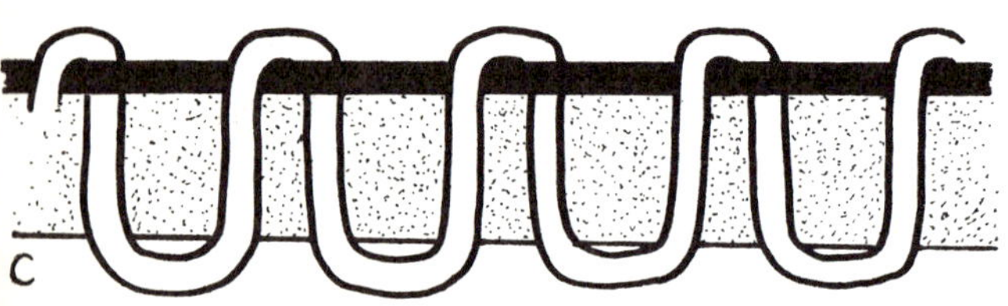

30. *Three kinds of tension. A. Normal tension (cross-section of stitch). The top thread, which is white, shows only on top of the fabric; the bottom thread, which is black, shows only on bottom. B. Bottom tension tighter than top: top thread is pulled down. C. Top tension tighter than bottom: bottom thread is pulled up.*

Lesson 4: Stitch Variations From Tension Changes

Tension change is the great universal no-no of sewing machine dealers, yet it adds an entirely new and important dimension to creative machine embroidery. Once you overcome the mystique that has been built up about machine tension, once you learn exactly how tension works, there is no problem. Changing the upper tension on most machines is easy—it involves adjusting a dial or gauge for more (+) or less (-) tension. Bottom tension is usually adjusted by turning a small screw (see figure 35) on the bobbin case. Don't turn the screw very much at a time—it's very short. (Hold the case over a jar lid or box lid while you're experimenting—there's less danger of losing the screw.) Some very automatic machines have no bobbin adjustment; in this case use a darning setting, which bypasses tension completely. You should check your owner's manual for instructions on tension changes, since every machine is different, and also to learn about your particular darning setting.

NORMAL TENSION AND TENSION CHANGES

But before you start changing tension, you must first learn to recognize normal tension. Put contrasting colored threads top and bottom in your machine. Set the upper tension at normal. Using the normal dressmaking setting,* run several rows of straight stitches on a double thickness of fabric. Look at them carefully. The top thread should lie along the top of the fabric, the bottom thread along the bottom, with neither color showing on the opposite surface.

If the bottom color shows on top, the bottom tension is too loose—it's being pulled up by the tension on top. If the top color shows on the bottom, the bottom tension is too tight—it's pulling the top thread down. Make the necessary adjustments until the threads behave correctly. Take out the bobbin case and pull a bit of thread from the bobbin. Notice how it feels. Try to memorize the pull of normal tension. Practice this a bit until it becomes familiar. For those of you who will be doing a great deal of machine embroidery I would suggest buying an extra bobbin case. Then you will have one for regular sewing and one you can adjust for tension change when machine embroidering.

Practice changing the bobbin tension and returning it to normal until you feel reasonably familiar with the process. Now you are ready to experiment and to use bobbin-tension change as a creative tool. That's what it's there for.

You have experimented with the straight stitch and the zigzag stitch. There are two other distinctive stitches in machine embroidery: the whip stitch and the cable stitch.

WHIP STITCH

The whip stitch results when the top tension is tighter than the bottom tension, causing the bottom thread to be pulled up and whipped around the top thread. This creates a subtly different texture, and when contrasting colors of threads are used interesting color changes are possible. Try it—you'll like it.

EXERCISE 13. With the presser foot off, teeth down, bottom tension normal, top tension tighter, red thread on

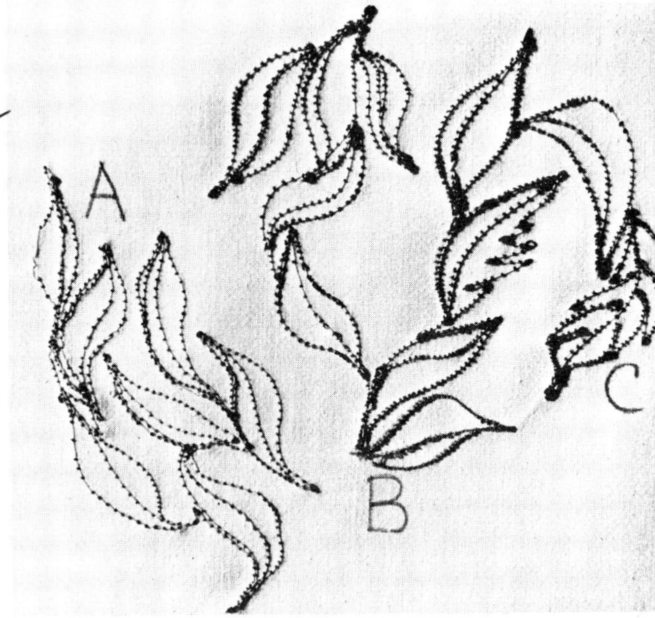

31. Whip stitch is formed when the top tension is tighter than the bottom tension. Here the black bottom thread is pulled up and whipped around the grey top thread, creating different textures. A. Top tension tightened, bottom tension normal. B. Top tension tightened, bottom tension slightly loosened. C. Top tension tightened, bottom tension quite loose. Notice the knot formed when the hoop's motion is arrested.

*A normal dressmaking setting means normal tension top and bottom, straight stitch, average stitch length (1½ to 2 on a scale of 4), teeth, presser foot, and no hoop. This is the combination necessary for a normal sewing stitch.

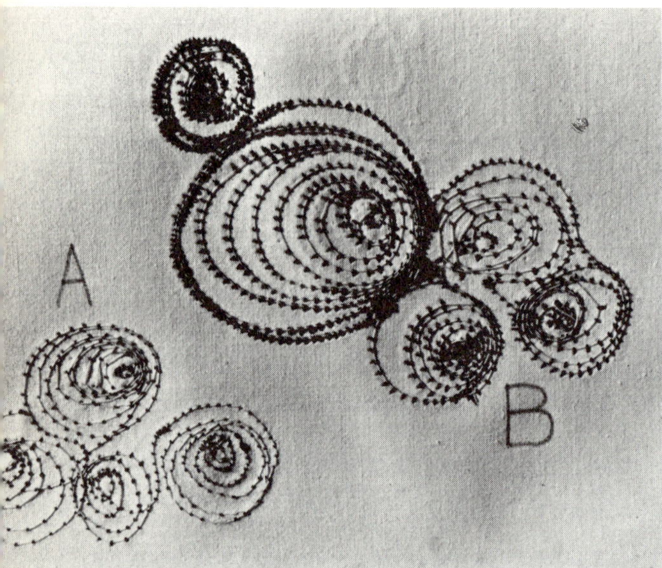

32. *Whip stitch worked quickly in tight circles forms small spikes, a technique used to create the impression of soft spring blossoms in figure C8. A. Top tension tightened, bottom tension normal. B. Top tension tightened, bottom tension loosened.*

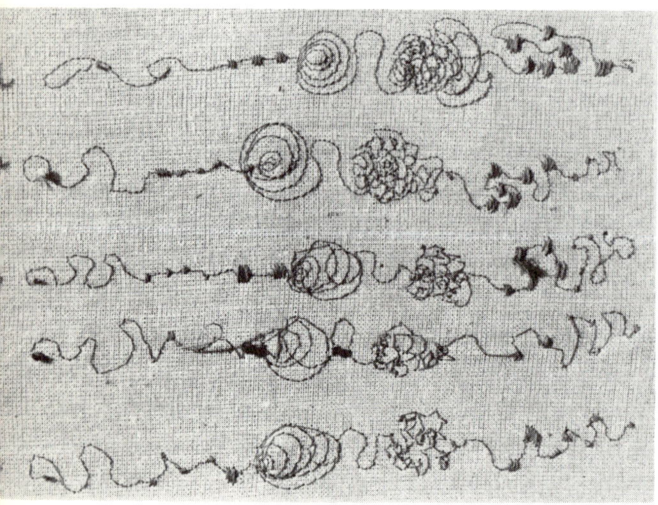

33. *Cable stitch: wrong (working) side. Top tension slightly loosened, regular sewing thread through the needle.*

top and yellow thread on the bottom, work an all-over pattern of small linear apple motifs, stitching each one quickly, capturing the essence of your apple's shape. Tighten the top tension a bit more. Be aware of the color change. Notice what happens when you run the machine faster, then slower. Notice what happens when you move the fabric faster, then slower. In other words, observe all the variations that can occur with this change in tension. Finish the pattern of apples (some should be red, some yellow, and some combinations of both colors). Put green leaves at the top of each apple.

Some machines are more responsive to tension change than others. If you notice little or no change when working the above exercise, loosen the lower tension slightly in addition to tightening the top tension. It is the relationship between top and bottom that makes the difference.

If you have not already done so, loosen the screw on the bobbin case about a quarter- or half-turn (or loosen the bottom tension control slightly). Experiment further with this tension relationship. Try some tight, fast little circles. Note the effect: if the fabric is moved swiftly in a circular pattern, the top tension is tightened even more, pulling up a pattern of little spikes of bobbin thread. This is a particularly nice texture for woolly sheep, spring blossoms, and other soft things (see figure C8).

EXERCISE 14. Starting from the center and working out in fast, concentric circles, create an apple shape in whip stitch.

EXERCISE 15. Sketch a large apple with chalk. Fill in half the negative (background) area with whip stitch (we'll fill the other half later). Vary the speed of the machine and the speed of the fabric to create different color effects. Create interesting patterns of stitched and nonstitched areas. Here you are creating texture as well as pattern.

CABLE STITCH

The cable stitch also involves tension change, but for a different reason. The cable stitch is worked from the wrong side of the piece, hence the bobbin thread becomes the top thread, allowing you to use a heavier thread than would go through the eye of a needle. With the tension loosened considerably, single-ply Persian wool, No. 5 perle cotton, or medium-weight crochet cotton will pass through the bobbin. With the spring bypassed (see figure 35) you can use even heavier threads—Bella Donna, No. 3 perle cotton. This adds an entirely new dimension to the texture of machine embroidery.

Most heavier threads can be wound on the bobbin in the regular way. A pencil can serve as a longer, hand-held thread spindle for crochet-cotton balls. Extra-heavy threads can be wound by hand.

EXERCISE 16. Fill in the remainder of the negative area in the preceding exercise with cable stitch. Work from the wrong side and use medium-weight crochet cotton (or something similar) in the bobbin. Loosen the bobbin tension just enough to allow the heavier thread the same amount of pull that you determined before to be normal tension. Change the effect of your stitch by varying the speed of your machine and the speed at which you move the fabric. Experiment with both straight and zigzag here; you'll find this rather exciting because you can't tell what's happening until you turn your fabric over.

The cable stitch makes it easy to stitch a particular pattern or design because the design can be transferred or drawn (in reverse) on the back of the fabric. Since the stitching is worked from the back side, the transfer marks won't show after the piece is worked.

EXERCISE 17. On the back of a piece of unbleached muslin, draw an apple tree. Work the apples in cable stitch in concentric circles of red thread on top and red one-ply Persian wool in the bobbin. Work green leaf textures around the apples by changing to green No. 5 perle cotton in the bobbin. Fill with a small, closely worked pattern (see figure 34B), that doubles back on itself, piling up a rough, leaflike texture on the wrong side (which is really the right side). For an autumnal tree, autumn golds, reds, and browns can be mixed with the greens. The trunk of the tree may be worked

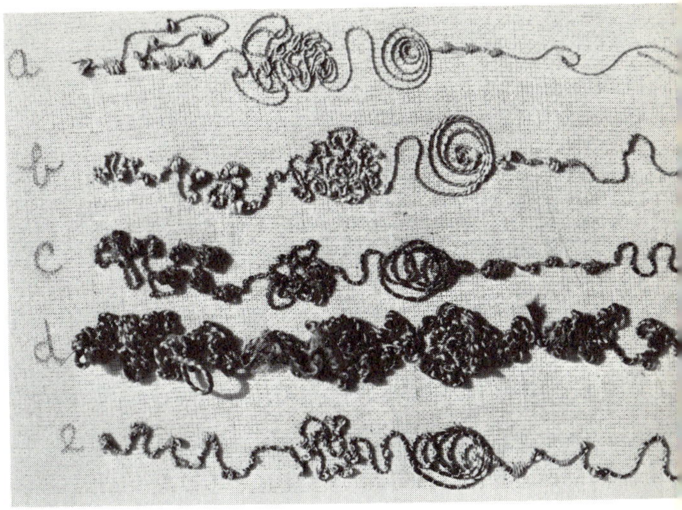

34. Cable stitch: right (bobbin) side of figure 33, showing five examples of how the type of thread changes the nature of a row of stitching. A. Button twist in bobbin, bottom tension slightly relaxed. B. No. 5 perle cotton in bobbin, tension loosened slightly. C. One-ply Persian wool in bobbin, tension same as for B. D. No. 3 perle cotton in bobbin, bobbin tension spring bypassed. E. Rayon thread in bobbin, tension same as for B. and C.

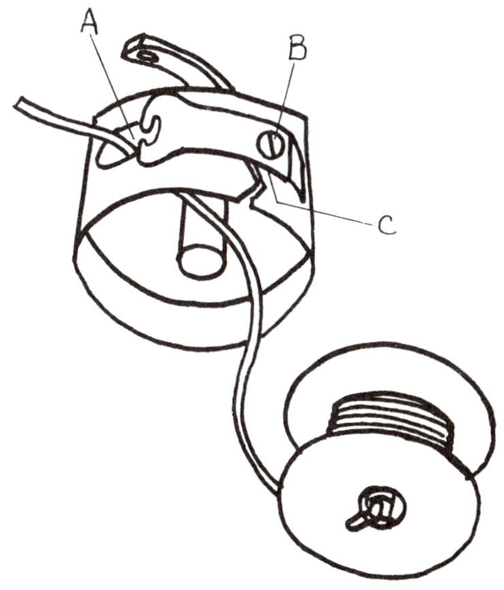

35. Bypassing the bobbin-tension spring. A. Large opening. B. Spring screw. C. Tension spring.

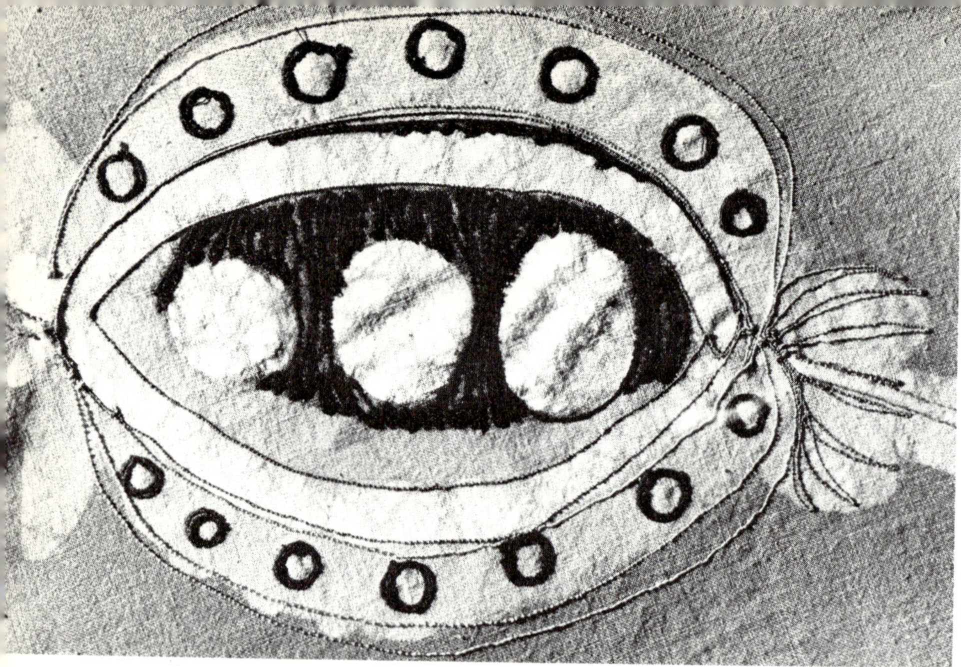

36. *Here whip stitch is used to enhance the texture of a batik design. Notice the beaded effect of the stitching.*

37. *Whip stitch enriches the neckline of the batiked caftan shown in figure C13.*

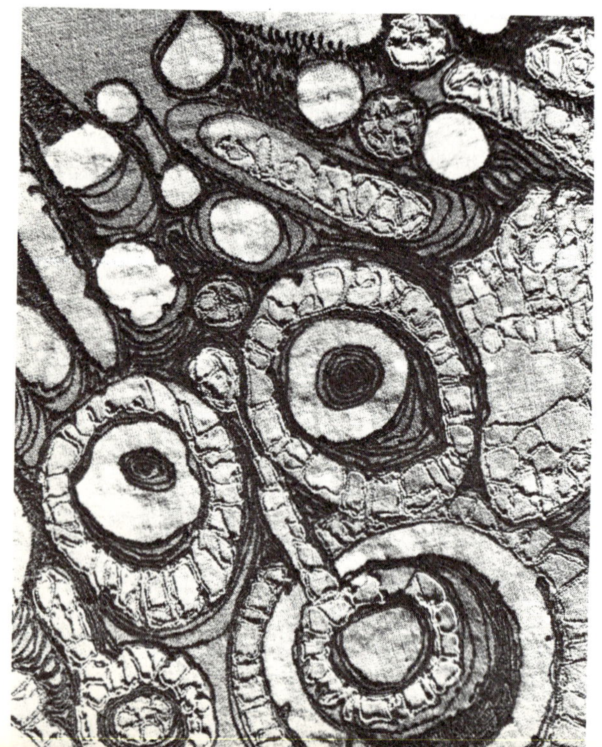

with heavier brown threads in the bobbin and a rough, jagged motion as in figure 40, creating a barklike texture. Remember, the bottom side (bobbin side) is the right side. Save this sampler.

WHIP-STITCH AND CABLE-STITCH PROJECTS

The following are projects to try once you feel you have mastered the whip stitch and the cable stitch.

A. Using normal-weight thread, put green thread on top and yellow thread in the bobbin. Have a red bobbin in reserve. Set the top tension at normal, loosen the bottom tension slightly. By changing only the top tension from normal to slightly looser to slightly tighter, and using both bobbins, create an overall pattern of autumn leaves as they would appear turning from green to yellow to red.

B. Enrich the texture of a commercially printed fabric (or a piece you have printed or batiked) with texture created by using heavy shiny thread (such as No. 3 or No. 5 perle cotton or Bella Donna) in the bobbin, worked from the wrong side in cable stitch. Accent this texture with regular free-machined lines.

30

38. *Spiked circles made by pulling down the top thread of the cable stitch (upper and lower right). Center: bobbin thread removed so the spikes are not connected.*

39. *More whip stitch on batik. Note the pin-tucked line (left) worked with the double needle (joining embellishment A, page 52).*

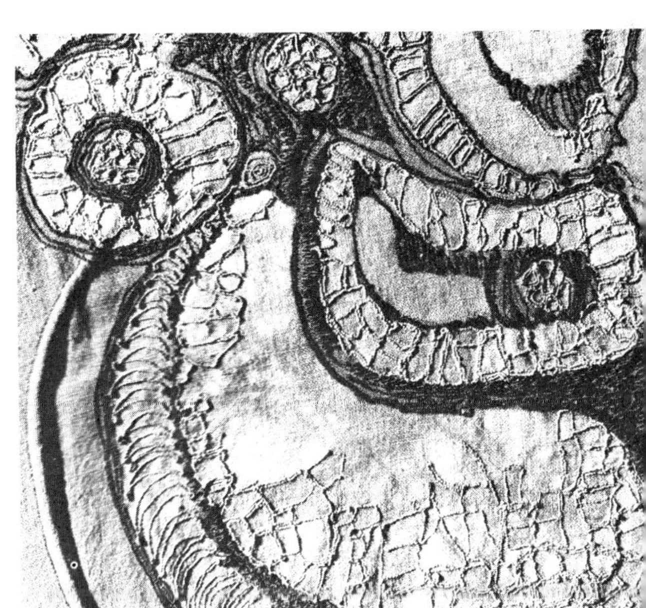

C. Create an elegant white-on-white design with a variety of threads in the bobbin. Draw the design on the wrong side of the fabric and stitch from that side with cable stitch. Use zigzag as well as straight stitch and concentrate on piling up heavy textures with closely spaced stitching. Allow the white fabric to play an important part in your composition as a contrast to the textured stitches.

D. Experiment with the spiked circles mentioned in connection with whip stitch (exercise 13, final paragraph.) Work some circles from the wrong side with cable stitch; you will find the spiked effect is heightened through the use of heavier thread in the bobbin. Secure the stitches on the wrong side by painting the fabric with white glue, or bonding them with iron-on Pellon or transparent food wrap. (If you bond the stitches with food wrap, use a paper towel between the wrap and your iron, which should be set for the heat required for your material, but in any case must be hot enough to melt the food wrap.) Then carefully remove the connecting (bobbin) thread with tweezers, leaving only the spikes. By varying the concentration of these stitches through the speed of fabric and overstitching, you can get unusual textural effects.

40. *Knots are formed by allowing thread to pile up in place under the needle.*

Lesson 5: Creating New Textures

Texture is perhaps the most distinctive element of embroidery composition. Texture is the surface feel: rough or smooth, matte or shiny, soft or hard. Embroidery, more than most other art forms, cries out to be felt: it is a tactile medium. And machine embroidery is no exception—any time thread is applied to fabric, textural change, to a small or large degree, is created. If you examine your previous samples you will see that the threads you applied to the fabric create different types of texture. The whip and cable stitches of Lesson 4 have a different surface feel from the more regular lines of Lesson 3. It is often a very subtle difference, but a difference nonetheless.

KNOTS

Machine-formed knots may be compared to hand-embroidered French knots, and like French knots may suddenly disappear to the underside of the fabric if pulled too tightly or formed on a fabric that is too openly woven. A knot is formed by simply pausing and allowing thread to pile up in one particular spot, although sometimes a very slight circular motion on the spot is necessary.

Prepare to work knots by loosening the bottom and top tensions slightly, framing up a piece of fabric, and setting the stitch width at 0. Move the fabric in a rapid up-and-down motion forming rows of narrow, bladelike shapes, pausing briefly at the top and bottom of each point.

A small, firm knot will form each time the motion is arrested. Do the same experiment with different-colored threads top and bottom. Do you notice any color change between the knots and the lines? Any color change related to the speed with which you move the hoop? Consider how you can make use of this in your samples.

EXERCISE 18. Create a small apple filled with knots, using red thread on top, yellow thread below. Work this on a dark fabric (dark green, brown, or black) and allow some of the fabric to show (this will be the darker values of the apple). Place the knots close together or far apart so that the value difference will suggest the basic contours of the apple—dark where the apple curves away from the light, light where the apple curves up into the light. This building up of lights and darks through small knots is called *seeding* or *powdering*. Entire areas may be worked in this way. Knots make a nice contrast to the smoother textures of line and satin stitch.

BLOBS

A more obvious form of texture is accomplished through forming blobs. Blobs, like knots, are formed by stopping the motion of the hoop, but this time a zigzag stitch is used—1 through 4, depending upon the size of the blob desired. It is worked in fits and starts—pausing to build up the blob, then moving the hoop *very* quickly to the next position and pausing again, which results in heavy blobs of thread joined by zigzags (see figure 41).

To make blobs, loosen the top and bottom tensions slightly and use contrasting colored threads top and bottom. Set the stitch width at 4 and frame up your fabric. Begin by zigzagging five or six strokes in one place, building up a pile of thread. Move very quickly in one rapid motion to another place and pause, building up another blob. (Caution: be sure to run your machine at a very rapid rate to avoid catching the needle in the fabric while moving from one blob to another; this will prevent needle breakage).

41. Blobs—in this case worked in cable stitch to form a heavier textured effect.

42. Blobs; blobs and loops; blobs with loops cut off.

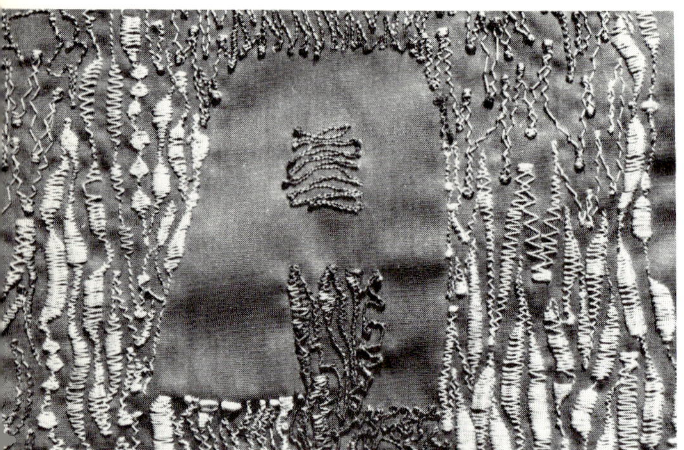

43. *Negative (unstitched) area forms a letter A; the positive (stitched) area is filled with knots, blobs, and manually adjusted thick-and-thin lines.*

44. *Couching with heavy rug yarn (far left) knotted and bunched under the needle, and (center left) laid in rows and couched to fill the area. The right side of the apple has whip-stitched circles.*

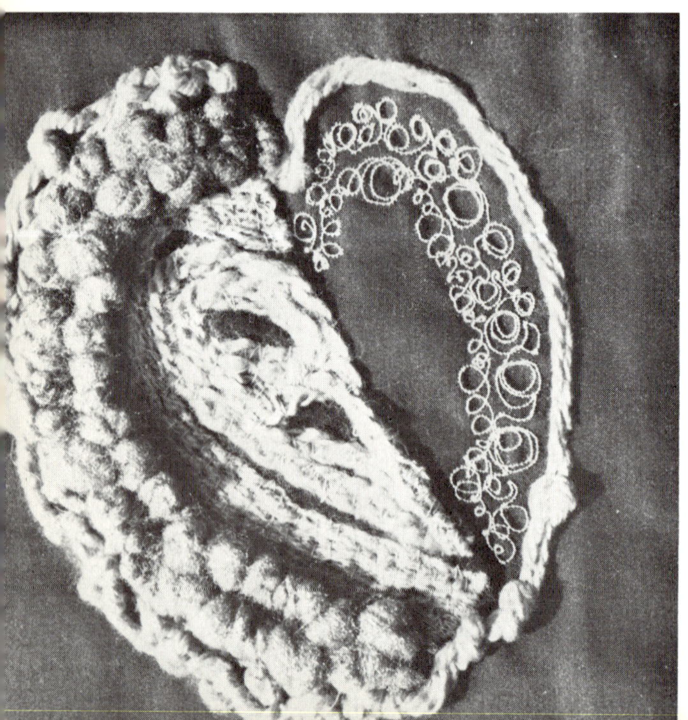

Repeat this, creating a seeding pattern of blobs connected by widely spaced zigzag.

If you want only the blobs (without the joining threads), work in the following manner: zigzag in place to build up a blob, then, without moving the fabric, adjust the stitch width to 0 and lock the blob by stitching in place for two or three stitches. Pause with the needle raised and loop the thread between the needle and the blob around your left index finger. Move to the next blob position with the thread still looped around your finger. Straight stitch up and down several times before dropping the thread from around your finger. Switch the stitch width to 4 and build up a blob as before. Again anchor the blob with several straight stitches and repeat the sequence. On some machines it is best to raise the presser-foot bar before moving from one blob to another, especially if they are wide apart; this reduces pull on both the tension mechanism and the needle. As you can see, now your blobs are connected not by widely spaced zigzag but by one large loop of thread which can easily be cut off. Straight stitching in place at the beginning and end of the blob prevents it from pulling out after the intervening thread is clipped. These individual blobs may be spaced quite close together or wide apart, depending upon the dictates of your design. For an additional change in texture, retain rather than clip the large loops of thread. Knots and blobs can also be worked in cable stitch from the wrong side of the fabric. With heavier thread the knots become even larger.

EXERCISE 19. Frame up a plain piece of red fabric and with chalk draw a large block letter A (for apple). Loosen your top and bottom tensions slightly. In this sample we'll reverse the normal concept of positive and negative areas; the red fabric will become the positive area (the letter **A**), and will remain unstitched. Create a textured negative area around the **A** through closely worked patterns of knots and blobs combined with thick-and-thin zigzag lines (see exercise 11, page 22). Concentrate on creating an interesting overall pattern of textured stitches in contrast to the simple unstitched **A**. (Don't forget to stitch the center of the **A**.) Concentration of stitches plays an important part in the overall design as well as in the color of the piece (see figure 43). Save this sampler.

COUCHING

An even more obvious way to create texture in machine embroidery is through couching. To couch means to tie or fasten down. To couch, the embroiderer uses a variety of machine stitches to fasten a variety of threads to a piece of fabric. Here threads can be used that would never go through the eye of a needle—heavy rug yarn, thick-and-thin knitting yarn, knotted and braided threads, roving (those lovely unspun strands of fiber that look like Rapunzel's hair), and strips of cut and raveled fabric, to name only a few. Here the imagination can run riot—and should! Play with your threads and devise new and unusual combinations to couch. String wooden beads on heavy rug yarn with knots separating the beads at interesting intervals (apple seeds, perhaps?); untwist heavy woolen yarn and spread the strands to cover an area. Then try to imagine just what kind of machine stitching would best carry out the effect you wish to achieve.

Following is a list of ways to use couching. I'm sure you can think of more.

A. Use widely spaced, random zigzag to couch down raveled wool yarn that is spread and fanned out to cover an area. Work in the hoop.

B. Cover a heavy jute cord with closely spaced zigzag stitches (use the quilting or darning foot for this—it helps stabilize the cord). Again, work in the hoop.

C. Intermittently couch a heavy, soft yarn. There are two ways to do this. If you have a blind-hemming automatic cam stitch (consult your manual—not all machines have this feature) use an off-center needle. This couches only at widely spaced intervals and the yarn remains soft and fluffy rather than completely tacked down. Use the preser foot and teeth, no hoop, and an average stitch length.

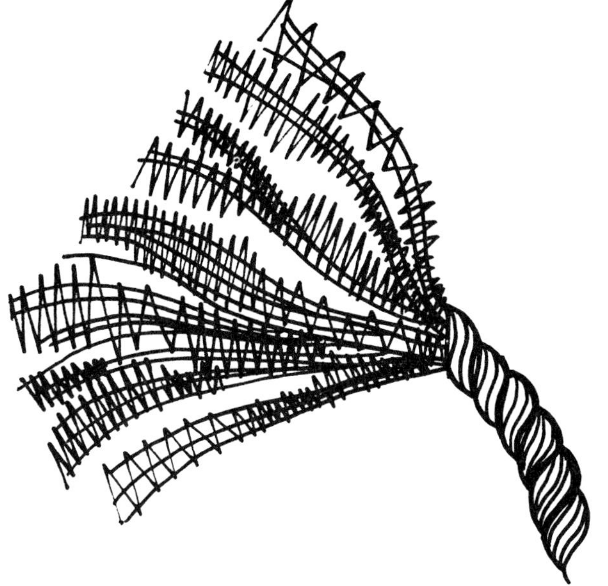

45. Varied stitch width and stitch concentration on raveled yarn.

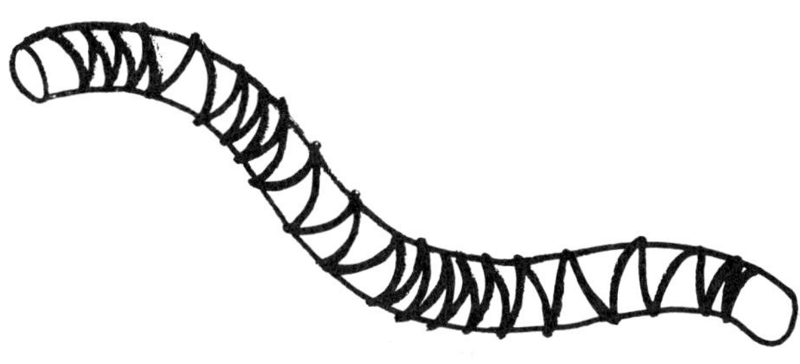

46. Varied stitch concentration on couched cord.

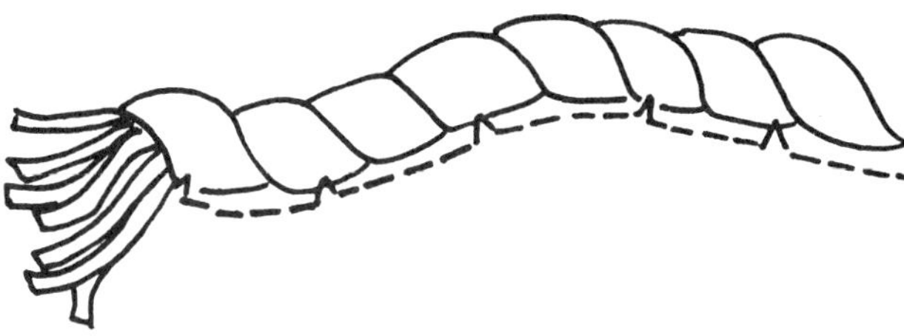

47. Yarn couched with a blind-hemming automatic cam stitch.

48. *Knotted rug yarn strung with beads and couched by free-machined straight stitching.*

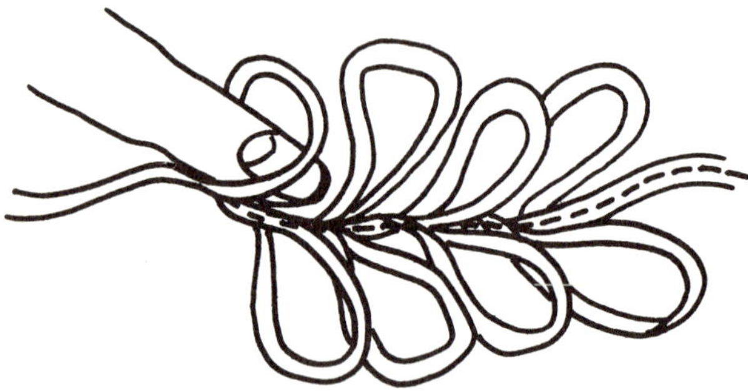

49. *Couched loops of yarn. For variety, change height and spacing of loops.*

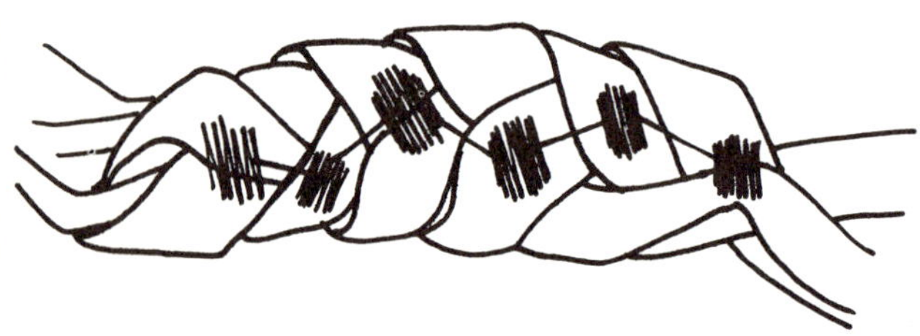

50. *Braid couched at the points where the three strips meet.*

If you do not have a blind-hemming setting, set the machine for free embroidering, using the hoop and no teeth. Straight stitch along the yarn, and at intervals move the fabric quickly, with a small jerk, to bring the yarn under the needle for one stitch only. Repeat this one-stitch couching as desired.

D. Combine beads with knots on a heavy rug yarn and couch with straight free machining, working around the knots and beads. Use the hoop for this, but no teeth.

E. Loop heavy rug yarn over a pencil or your finger and couch at the low point of the loops, leaving a high, raised texture. Use the hoop and free machining. The loops can be left as they are or clipped and contoured.

F. Braid three heavy strips of yarn or fabric together and couch with blobs at the join of each braid unit. Use the hoop and free machining.

Again, these are only a few suggestions for you to try. Once started, you'll undoubtedly invent couching methods of your own.

TEXTURE PROJECTS

In order to further explore the use of texture, you might like to try the following projects.

A. Study a striated textured object such as a slice of agate or a section of tree bark or a log. Stitch a composition suggestive of one of these by using couched heavy yarns combined with cable-stitched knots and blobs.

B. Stitch a stylized, geometric border design using only blobs and their connecting threads (threads that result from raising the presser foot bar and moving the hoop into position for the next blob). Devise interesting ways of couching down these connecting threads to form a further design. Combine this technique with automatic cam stitches if your machine has that feature.

C. Collect odds and ends of the threads and fabrics used in samples from this lesson—jute cord, rug yarn, fabric, beads, whatever. Ravel and shred some fabric pieces, tie knots in some of the yarn, and ravel other yarn. In other words, distort and change the remainders at hand. Frame up a piece of fabric and begin arranging this hodgepodge of textures in an interesting fashion within the circle of your hoop. Arrange and rearrange these bits and pieces until they please you from the standpoint of color, texture, value, and overall composition. Throw in other textures if you wish—nut shells, rice, beans—whatever appeals to you. When you are pleased with your "textural soup," pin a piece of nylon hose over the entire area. Cut through the nylon in places, pull some of your odds and ends of threads and materials through the holes, and generally play with the textures. Then free machine down what is necessary but, above all, use your machine to enhance, reiterate in stitches, and add to the textural interest of the collage you've created.

51. Left: bark of a tree. Right: heavy rug yarn, raveled fabric, and knotted threads, all couched to suggest the texture of the bark.

52. *Waled satin stitch suggests, among other things, the striped fur of a cat. See also the Pink Panther Tunic, figure C4.*

Lesson 6: Area, Value, Volume — Adding a Third Dimension

AREA

Area is the space bounded by a line. It defines shape, such as an apple or a leaf; it adds body and substance to a composition. You have already discovered one way of filling an area through the use of powdered or seeded knots. As in hand embroidery, perhaps the most common method of filling an area is by satin stitch.

SATIN STITCH

Satin stitch can be worked on the machine, either with or without the teeth and the presser foot. For a regular line no wider than the widest swing of the needle, the presser foot and teeth are recommended. No hoop is needed. Use an embroidery foot that has a wide groove on the bottom; this prevents close stitching from bunching up under the foot and causing stalls and unsightly blobs of thread. Relax the tensions slightly, particularly for lighter-weight fabric, and set the stitch length between 0 and 1. Width can be controlled manually. This stitch sometimes puckers lighter-weight fabrics. When that happens, either back the fabric with organdy or iron-on Pellon, or stitch with a piece of typing paper underneath the fabric. This works nicely for long, gently curving tendrils and anywhere an exact, carefully controlled line is desired.

Free satin stitch is done without the teeth or the presser foot, with the fabric in a frame, and the spacing controlled through the movement of the hoop. This requires practice, but once you've become adept you'll find the stitch is wonderfully versatile and not limited by the width of the needle swing.

Waled Satin Stitch

There are basically two ways that free satin stitch can be used to fill an area. One is simply to stitch rows of closely spaced zigzag lined up side by side (see figure 53) to form a waled or corded texture. This can be very effective when used to describe specific movement within an area: flowing water, patterns of cloud formations, the contours of grassy fields, rough bark textures, or the striped fur of a cat.

Encroaching Satin Stitch

The second method of filling an area with satin stitch is by "scumbling": stitching lightly in zigzag over the entire surface, spacing the stitches wide apart, much after the fashion of a painter who uses a thin turpentine wash to indicate the colors and values of an area. Move the zigzag swiftly and evenly over the fabric, gradually building up solid stitching by going over and over the area. Avoid uneven build-up, which could cause your machine to skip stitches when the needle moves from a solidly stitched area to one with lighter stitching. In effect, these stitches are encroached or laid within each other like interlocking teeth (figure 54). This results in an even, overall effect rather than definite lines of zigzag.

Exercise 20. With chalk, draw a large apple leaf (figure 55), clearly indicating the lines and direction of the veins. Stitch this solidly with waled satin stitch, free machined, following the lines you have indicated. Notice how the depressions between the stitching form natural veins. With the teeth and an embroidery foot (no hoop), embroider a stem, beginning with the full swing width at the tree end of

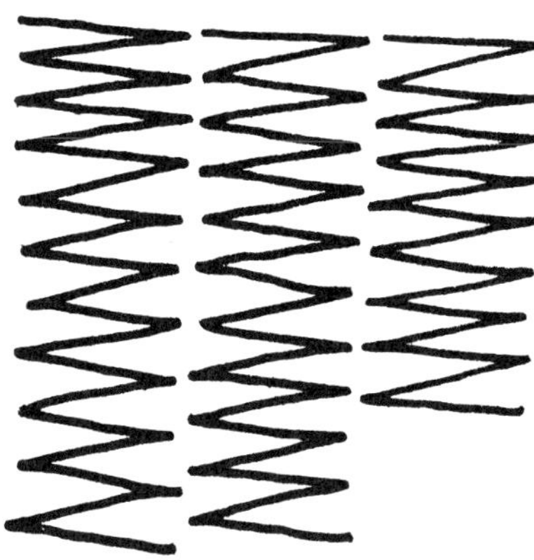

53. *Waled satin stitch. Space between stitches is exaggerated for clarity.*

54. *Encroaching satin stitch. Space between stitches is exaggerated for clarity.*

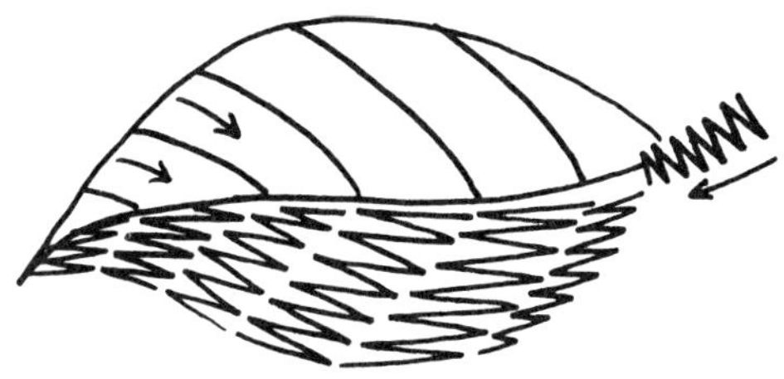

55. *Waled satin-stitched leaf.*

the stem, and gradually narrowing as the stem meets the leaf. You will find that any kind of embroidery causes some loss of form, so always make points more pointed and curves more curved for better definition of shape. Save this sample.

VALUE

The apple leaf that you have just stitched involved a flat leaf-shaped area defined by stylized vein lines. No attempt was made to show contours or curves through the use of light and dark areas (values) or shading. Value, a very important element of composition, is the lightness or darkness of an area, and usually results from the inclusion of yet another element of composition, volume.

VOLUME

Volume adds a third dimension to an otherwise two-dimensional medium. For the most part we have been dealing only with flat fabric having width and length. A third dimension, volume, may be added, either actually (by building up very heavy textures or high padded areas to contrast with low, flat ones), or visually (by an optical illusion that *suggests* depth or a third dimension through changes in scale and values). In actuality and in representational art, objects appear larger the nearer they are to us, and appear smaller as they recede into the distance. Distant objects are behind closer ones, and for the most part close objects are lighter and seem to darken in value as they move into the distance: again, light colors advance, dark colors recede.

Carefully study your old friend the apple. Place it in front of you in a fixed position with a steady source of light and look at it closely. The apple is a volume existing in space: it has length, width, and depth; you could walk around it. Now half-close your eyes and squint at it. You will notice that certain areas suddenly appear darker than others, while some are quite light. Of course, you say, that's because of shadows. But there is a reason for those shadows; they are

56. *Unstitched lines between the rows of satin stitch are used to suggest veins in this waled satin-stitched leaf.*

the effect, not the cause. Pick up the apple and close your hands around it. Look at your fingers—are they straight or curved? They are curved, of course, as the apple itself is. Part of the apple curves toward the source of light (hence part of it appears lighter); other parts of it curve away from the source of light (the darker values). Notice how dark it appears down in the depression where the stem comes out. Notice also how light it appears on the upper rim. Notice too that it curves not only vertically but horizontally.

Logically, it is much easier to indicate curved surfaces by using curved lines. Remember that, when you begin satin stitching your apple. And—very important—remember that there is a sound reason for dark and light values: shading. The form and contours of the object, and the reaction of those contours to light, cause shadows. So study carefully the form of the object you are drawing or painting or stitching, and the lights and shadows will naturally follow.

Sometimes highlights and contrasting edges occur in an object. Using them can add life and sparkle to your embroidery, but be careful to use them sparingly and don't allow them to confuse the issue, which is the basic form of the object.

As you continue to look at your apple, note how it relates to its background. At some places it stands out in sharp contrast, in others it blends almost imperceptibly into the background. The former we call a sharp, or hard, edge, the latter a soft edge. When you start stitching your apple, notice the contrasting edges—dark against light and light against dark—and the soft edges, which blend into the background. All this will add life and vitality to your work.

EXERCISE 21. Let's stitch a realistic interpretation of your apple. Place the apple in a position so it can be easily studied. Frame up the fabric, put the teeth down, and take the presser foot off, for free machining. Study carefully the variety of colors in the apple. If it is a red one it will have at least three values of red, perhaps some yellow, probably some green, and maybe other colors as well; you'll most likely want brown or black or very dark green for accents, so have a full pallette of colors at hand. Squint at the apple to

57. Apple contours showing both the vertical and horizontal curves of the apple's surfaces.

determine where the dominant darks and lights occur. Note carefully the shape of the apple—is it round, oblong, or crooked? How much of it actually touches the base on which it rests? Does it lean toward you? Away from you? How tall is it in proportion to its width? How wide is the base in relation to the top? To the sides? It's the relationship of one area to another that helps you actually depict what you see. Train yourself to be aware.

After determining exactly what your apple looks like, use your basic-colored thread to draw the apple with your machine, as you did in exercise 5. You might even slightly exaggerate particular characteristics—a crooked left side even more crooked, a pointed base even more pointed. Then, with zigzag on 4, lightly scumble in the predominate color, without building up too much thread in any one area. Allow a good deal of fabric to show through (this might even be one of your apple colors, thus relating positive and negative areas more closely).

Remember what was said before about depicting curved contours with curved lines? Look at figure 57 again. Now, first using darker thread in your needle and then lighter, push back the areas that curve away from the light and bring forward those areas that curve toward the light, scumbling in lightly with encroaching satin stitch. Again—try not to build up the thread too heavily. Continue this pushing-back, pulling-forward process until you are satisfied that your apple actually gives the impression of existing in space with air all around it. Look for the contrasting edges, dark against light, light against dark, and very selectively stitch these edges with a straight stitch or a very narrow zigzag. Have you observed the soft edges as well? Does your apple curve in at the bottom where it meets the table? If not, push it back and under a bit more. Does the color look a bit lifeless? Remember complementary colors enrich, so add a touch of green to the darker areas.

Be constructively critical of yourself. That is an important aspect of creative embroidery. If you are not satisfied with your results (and you probably won't be for the first five or six attempts), try to determine just why you

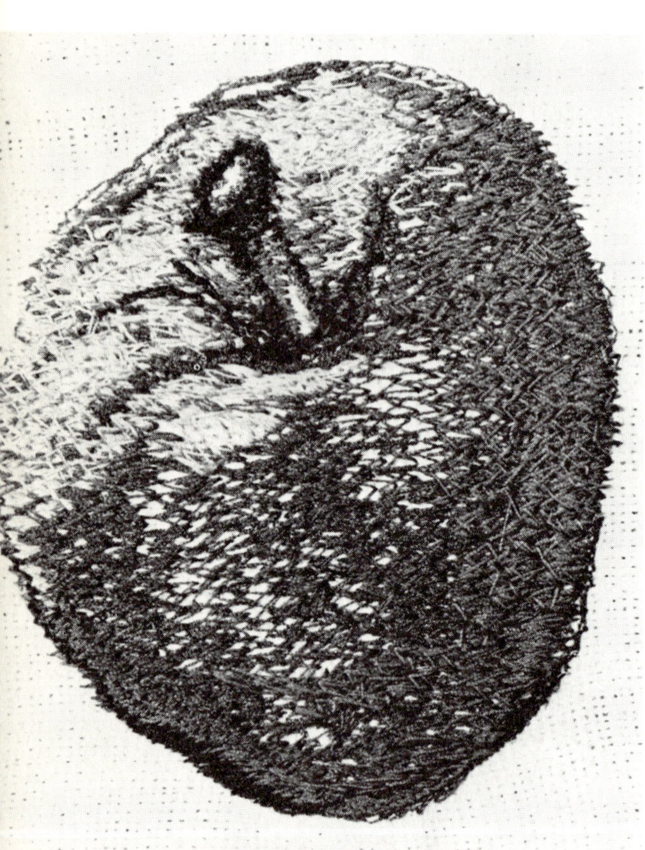

58. A realistically shaded apple, stitched in encroaching satin stitch.

are not satisfied, and what you can do to improve the piece. Then do several more samples, each time studying very carefully the features that were stressed above. Learn to look at the world through an embroiderer's eyes. Keep several of your most successful efforts.

APPLIQUÉ

One of the most delightful and versatile methods of filling an area is by appliqué, the applying of one fabric to another. This presents almost limitless possibilities because it involves not only a variety of threads but of fabrics as well. With appliqué, large areas can be created with a minimum of stitching, their variety limited only by your choice of fabrics. Sheers and nets can be overlaid and combined to make marvelous illusions, and applied fabrics can be stuffed, raised, contoured with quilting, and sculpted almost like clay. It is truly an exciting form of embroidery.

There are two basic methods of applying one fabric to another: from the back or from the front of the ground fabric. Each has its particular advantage.

Appliqué from the Back

This type of appliqué is used primarily when you wish to follow a specific pattern. Draw or transfer the pattern *in reverse* onto the back of the ground fabric, or pin a paper pattern to the back of the fabric, and stitch right through the paper, which is then pulled away. The fabric to be applied, roughly the size and shape of the pattern area, is basted or pinned or taped to the front of the ground fabric and framed up, and the design is free machine stitched from the reverse to mark the design. A narrow zigzag (1½ to 2) is best for this. The excess fabric is then carefully cut away from the front, leaving the basted appliqué. Finally, the edges are finished off as desired. This method is particularly good for lettering, which often requires precise spacing and delineation. For our next exercise we'll appliqué the word *apple* to another piece of fabric; for variety, let's arrange the letters vertically rather than horizontally (see figure 60).

59. *Preparation for appliqué from the back. A. Paper pattern, design in reverse. B. Ground fabric, wrong side up. C. Fabric to be applied, wrong side up.*

EXERCISE 22. Choose a piece of plain fabric for your ground. On the back of the fabric, in chalk, hard pencil, or permanent marking pen, draw in simple block letters the word *apple, in reverse*, reading from top to bottom. Or draw the letters, again in reverse, on a piece of paper, pinning it in place on the back side of the ground fabric. Remember that letters are like any other units of design. Space them in such a way that their weight has a pleasant distribution, negative areas are as carefully planned as positives, and, in addition, since they are letters, so that they are easy to read.

Choose a piece of harmonizing printed fabric a bit larger than the size of your entire word. Pin this in place face up on the *right* side of your fabric, making sure to cover the area of your word. For the best results, try to use the straight grain of both fabrics. Frame up both pieces of fabric (plus your paper pattern if you have one) for free machining on the side where the letters are drawn. Be sure the applied fabric is smooth and taut. With the zigzag set at 1½ or 2, stitch around all the letters. Remove the fabric from the hoop and pull away the paper pattern if you're using one. Turn the fabric to the right side. Your word is now clearly marked as well as basted in place. Remove the hoop, and with a pair of sharp scissors carefully cut away the excess fabric around each letter. If the scissors are held with the *palm of the hand up* there is less danger of clipping the stitching. Frame up again, right side up, and finish the edge of the letters with free-machined satin stitch (zigzag 3 or 4). Or use the teeth and the embroidery foot, and satin stitch around the letters. No hoop is necessary for the latter method.

Appliqué from the Front

If a simple flat shape is to be applied to the fabric, you may want first to bond it to the ground fabric. Place a small piece of plastic wrap or Stitch Witchery (a commercial bonding agent) between the piece to be applied and the ground fabric, and press with a moderate iron. When heat is applied the plastic melts, fusing the two fabrics together. Be sure the plastic wrap doesn't come into direct contact with

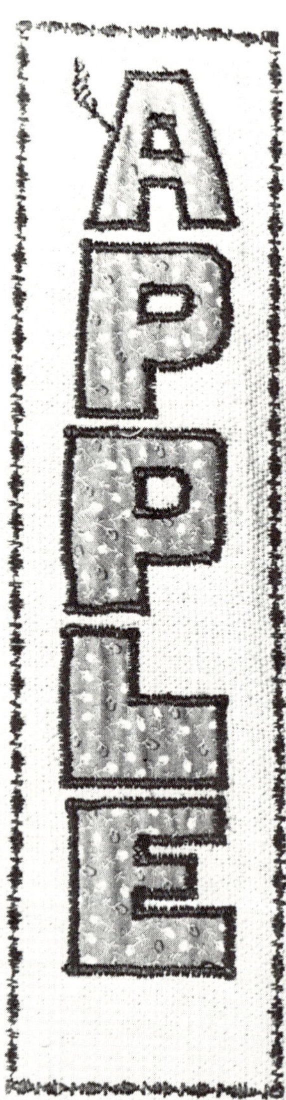

60. *Finished appliqué done from the back: hard edges are finished with satin stitch, using the presser foot and teeth.*

C1. *Nomad dress.*

C2. *Detail of nomad dress.*

C3. *Blue denim tote.*

C4. *Pink Panther Tunic.*

C5. *Inside top of Elemental Box.*

C6. Autumn detail of Four Seasons Caftan.

C7. Four Seasons Caftan.

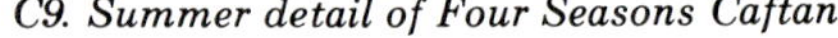

C8. Spring detail of Four Seasons Caftan.

C9. Summer detail of Four Seasons Caftan.

C10. Shag bag.

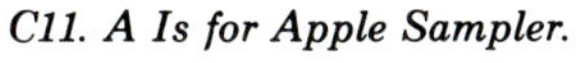

C11. *A Is for Apple Sampler.*

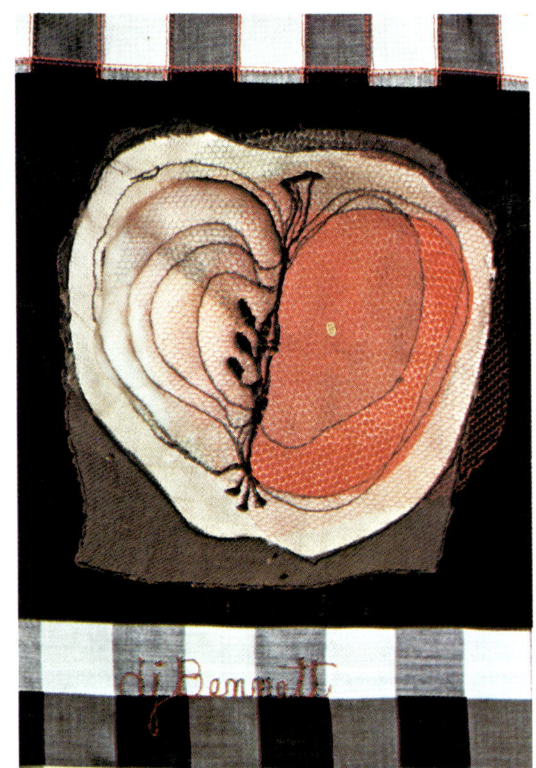

C12. *Detail of sampler.*

C13. *Quilted caftan.*

C14. *Blue collar.*

C15. *Detail of Leopard Poncho (poncho itself shown on next page).*

C16. Leopard Poncho.

C17. Detail of needle-lace caftan.

C18. Elemental Box.

C19. Inside bottom of Elemental Box.

C20. Cat and Mouse Box.

the iron. With either bonding agent a slight stiffness will occur in the fabric.

Next, frame the two fabrics in a hoop for free machining and, with the zigzag set at 1 or 1½, stitch a row of widely spaced stitches around the apple shape. You can also do this without the hoop, using the embroidery foot and teeth if you desire. This serves as a preliminary basting stitch, much as it did in the preceding exercise. If a second apple shape is to be applied, overlapping part of this one, now is the time to do it, following the same procedure as for the first. When all overlapped shapes are basted into place, the edges are ready to be finished as you choose. You can use a hard, satin-stitched edge, this time closely spaced, with the zigzag set wider than 1½. Or you might finish with a soft edge— perhaps more widely spaced stitches to blend with those already there or with those in the surrounding area. Conversely, you might use heavier stitching in the negative area surrounding the apple as you did in exercise 19 (page 34), allowing the loosely stitched fabric edge to show. There is no one way of doing it. Don't hesitate to experiment with combinations of techniques that you've already learned.

Appliqué done from the front is most useful for areas that are to be overlapping or built up in stages, perhaps with several layers of fabric and some padding. In this situation it is a bit more difficult to control the fabric, which is often cut exactly to size and shape before the stitching is done. If padding is to be inserted under the applied fabric, bonding materials cannot be used. In any case, pin the applied fabric in place. An easy way to apply pieces of several different sizes and shapes is to arrange them under a layer of net or nylon hose; then only the net need be fastened with stitching, not each individual piece of fabric. Additional padding may be tucked in and other fabrics added as the stitching progresses, which results in a quite sculptural approach to embroidery. Figures 61 through 69 show the step-by-step progression of such an appliqué (complete with what not to do), and how errors can be corrected. Note how the values and textures of the piece change as the layers are added and changed.

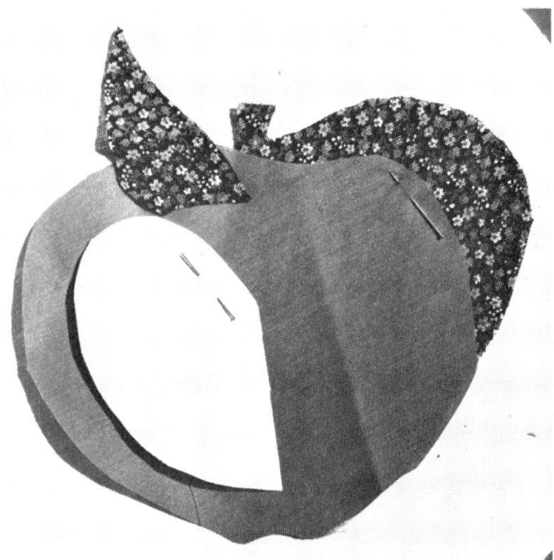

61. *Appliqué from the front: ground fabric in hoop; cut-out apple design pinned in position.*

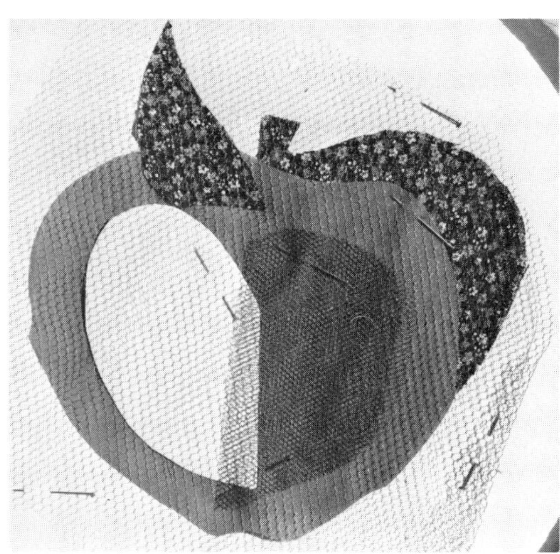

62. *Right half of the core area of an apple, cut from net and pinned in place on the right-hand side of the apple. Another piece of net covers the entire apple, extending beyond to create a slightly textured area around the apple.*

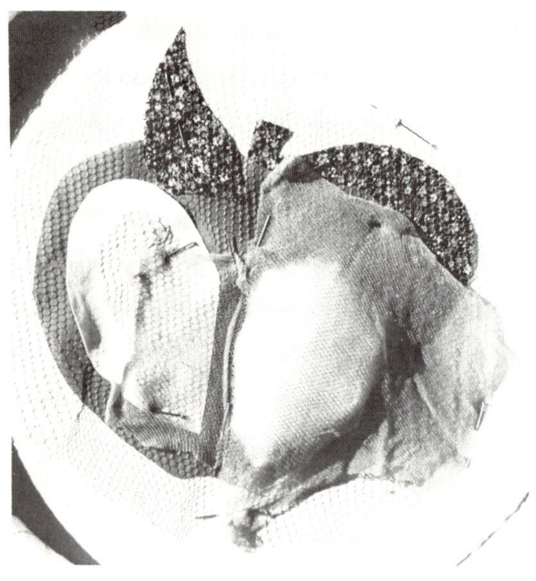

63. *Left side with part of the net cut away. Nylon hose is pinned over the right half and polyfill stuffing tucked underneath.*

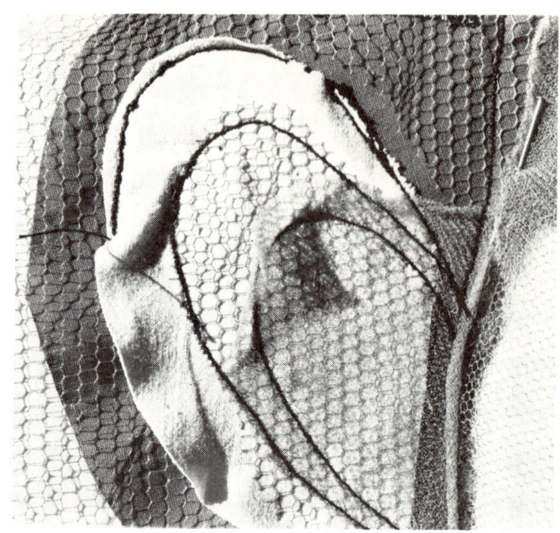

64. *Freely stitched lines begin to delineate the core. Note that the outer edge of the white area, where the net has been cut away, should have been fused with plastic or pinned securely before stitching was begun. The edge of the fabric stretched and moved out of place, resulting in an unsightly pucker. Notice too how the raw edge of nylon hose (center of core) has rolled, forming a definitive line that will be kept as part of the contour of the piece.*

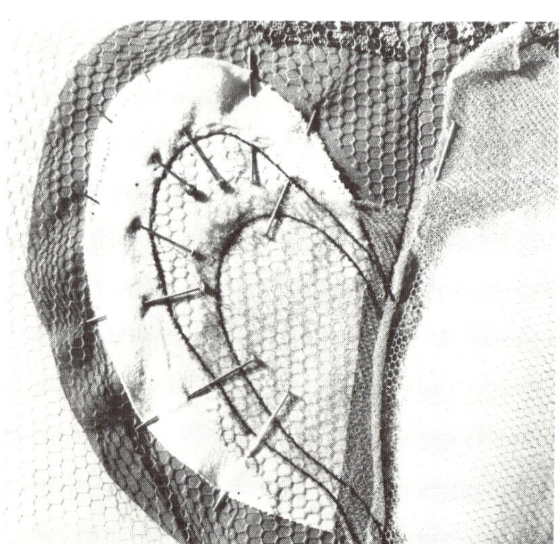

65. *Stitching has been removed from the puckered piece, and the problem edge securely pinned.*

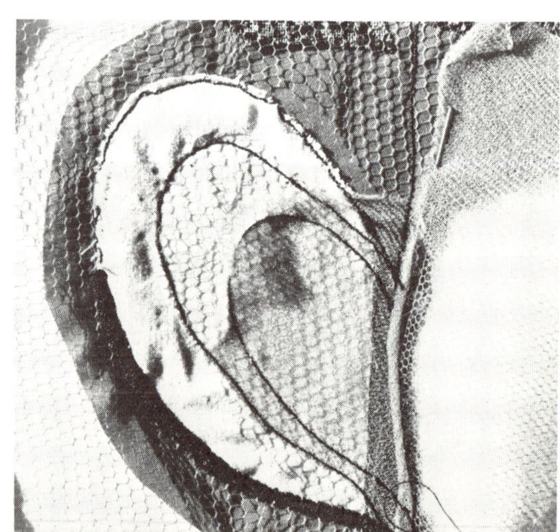

66. *A line of free basting stitch runs around the outer edge of the white. Dark satin stitching has been started from the bottom to cover the roughly basted edge.*

Hard edges may be finished with the same type of satin stitch just used, or perhaps you'd like to couch the edge with a heavy piece of rug yarn for added impact. Soft edges can be secured by interesting lines of free machining, either with straight or zigzag stitching. Free machining is particularly effective for use with nets, nylon hose, and other fragile fabrics not subject to raveling. It is important to plan your composition so that the stay stitching (the stitching that secures the applied fabrics to the ground fabric) becomes an integral part of the embroidery itself. The composition should have three equally important elements—the ground fabric, the applied fabric, and the stitching.

EXERCISE 23. Study the cut surface of half an apple. Notice particularly the pattern formed by the core and seeds. Notice too the delicate edge of peel. On a framed-up ground fabric, build up a three-dimensional stylized collage interpreting this half-apple. Cut a number of appropriate shapes from various colored nets, sheers, and lightweight fabrics, arranging them not only to make an apple shape, but to explore interesting color and value changes through different fabric combinations. Pad sections with polyfill by slipping the batting under areas you feel should be raised. Notice how texture changes when the nets are used at different angles. You might even lay on a few well-chosen beads for apple seeds. Then cover the entire collage with a piece of nylon hose. Notice the subtle richness the nylon gives to the other fabrics (it will hold them all in place as well). You might take advantage of the way in which edges of the nylon curl, making a sharper, heavier line. Pin everything in place, then embroider any details that you feel are necessary to make it definitely a half-apple and at the same time to hold the fabric in place. You'll find you can use free stitching right up to any beads you have placed under the nylon. Finish some sections with a hard edge, some soft, perhaps even working textured negative areas close enough to secure edges of the positive. Save this sample.

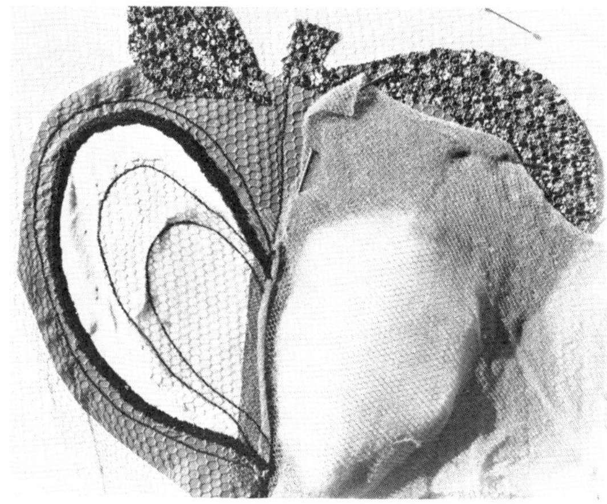

67. *The problem edge is finished with satin stitching.*

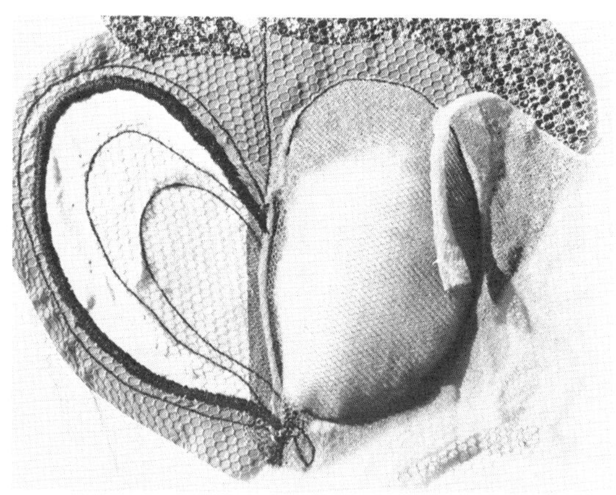

68. *The outer edge of the right-hand core is defined with a row of free stitching, and the excess nylon hose is cut away. Note the different textures resulting from net over net, and nylon over net.*

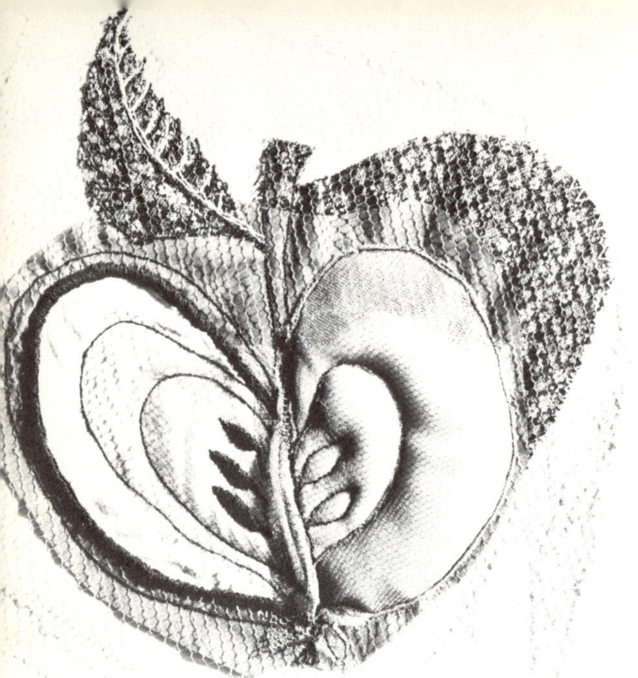

69. *The right-hand core is quilted with straight free machining, with seeds adding to the quilted contours. The seeds on the left were worked in free-machined satin stitch. Vein lines have been added to the leaf.*

70. *A different interpretation of the same theme, appliquéd from the front. Notice the soft edges created by overlapping layers of net.*

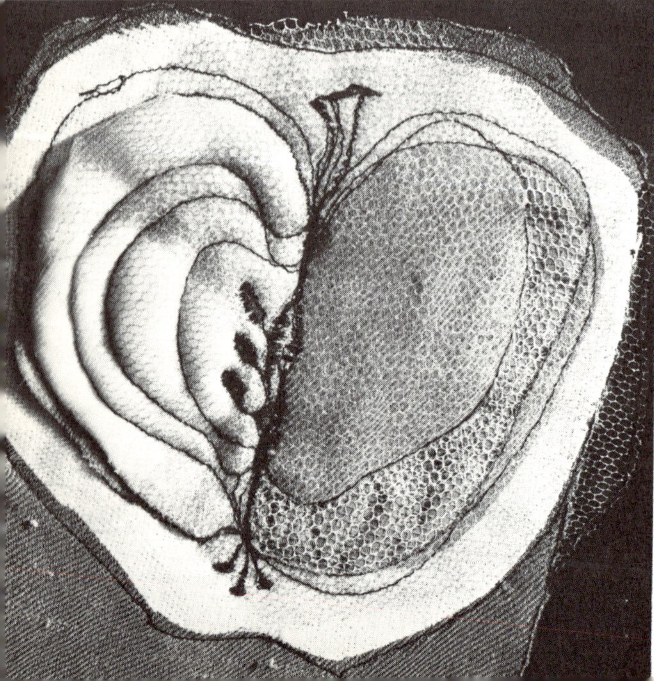

APPLIQUÉ AND THREE-DIMENSIONAL PROJECTS

Following are some projects you might like to try after you have completed the exercises in this lesson.

A. Using the pattern and directions for making a tote bag, page 58, make a monogrammed bag featuring a three-initial monogram appliquéd from the wrong side. Plan your letters carefully to best suit the size and shape of the bag, and make them big, bold, and dramatic. Try to relate the fabric of the letters to other areas of the bag so they add to the composition as a whole. Finish the appliqué before constructing the bag.

B. Work another version of exercise 21 (page 41), but this time put darker or lighter thread in the bobbin. Get the necessary value variations by changing the top tension, using both top and bottom thread colors as well as the color of the fabric to create the apple form.

C. Make interesting values and contours with layers of nylon hose over dacron polyfill. Experiment with a composition of closely spaced faces in a crowd, working the layers of fabric with free machining. Work either with a hoop and no foot or without a hoop using the darning (quilting) foot. Use a fairly stable fabric—heavy muslin, denim, or drapery material—as ground fabric for this piece.

Lesson 7: Creative Joinings— A Finished Sampler

ARRANGING THE SAMPLES

By now you have been introduced to the basic techniques of machine embroidery. You have created twenty or more samples of different styles, shapes, and sizes illustrating these techniques, and all are related in some way to the apple. The next problem is to put the samples together in a pleasing, well-designed wall hanging. The hanging, as a good composition, should—to repeat what I said in Lesson 2—hold together, be interesting to look at, and have a pleasing relationship between positive and negative areas. Your samples are the positive (stitched) areas. The joinings, the fabric in between the samples, are the negative. And it is primarily with those that you will be involved in this lesson.

You'll be using checked gingham to unify the composition and join the samples into a rectangular panel; at the same time you can experiment with pieces of gingham as individual projects in themselves. There are several reasons for using checked gingham. The regularity of the check will aid in joining the different-sized and -shaped samples into the rectangle. At the same time, the check lends itself well to all kinds of fabric manipulation, development of repetitive motifs, and pattern change.

71. *Finished A Is for Apple Sampler with various treatments of checked joinings. See also C11.*

The first step of the project is to place your samples face down on terrycloth toweling and lightly press them, steaming gently and pulling them into shape if necessary. Press lightly so that the stitching is not flattened. Raise padded areas by holding the iron an inch or two above the surface of the right side and fluffing them with steam. Next, allowing plenty of floor space, spread your samples out to form an oversize rectangular patchwork. This gives you a chance not only to view them collectively, but to determine roughly how many pieces you have and approximately how large your final sampler will be. Remember, the overall size will be reduced a good deal by seaming and cropping. Don't be alarmed if they don't all fit well together—that's the whole point of the joining problem. Move the samples around a bit, concentrating on good color distribution (don't have all the strong reds in one spot, or all the delicate little linear drawings grouped together). Try for variety as well as balance in both color and value. Half-close your eyes to see if the darks and lights flow smoothly throughout the piece. Don't worry if the units aren't all the same size—they shouldn't be. Two small pieces side by side can relieve the solidity and sameness of one large one. Some samples will be long and narrow, some will be square, some round, some wider than high. That's all for the good; it adds interest and variety to your piece. Be sure to include one sample of your name so your work will be signed.

When you have arranged the samples in a relatively satisfactory composition (and remember, nothing is final at this stage), start critically examining each area for size and shape. Is one sample lost in a sea of negative space? If so, try turning under some of the fabric and cropping it. Is one motif too close to an edge? Cut it out and apply it to another fabric. Experiment with different proportions and press under any fabric you feel is superfluous. Some designs look better with negative space around them; some are more interesting if allowed to bleed right off the ground fabric. Play with these relationships until you are satisfied with the results, remembering all the while that you will be adding strips of gingham at strategic spots.

72. *Samples joined in a vertical strip, with checked gingham joinings.*

Now, with the samples still arranged in front of you, begin to play with the gingham itself. Estimate what the dimensions of the sampler will be and reserve for the sampler backing a piece of gingham the same height as the sampler and 3 inches wider on each side. You'll also need to reserve gingham for finishing the top and bottom of the sampler—these pieces should be 3 inches less in width than the backing you just cut, with one piece 5 inches high, the other 7.

With the remainder of the gingham you'll be making a variety of joining strips to go between the samples. Plan for variation of width in these joinings as well as variation of treatment. Your samples will be joined together first in vertical strips, with gingham joinings added where necessary to make them all one width (see figure 72). Plan at least three or four vertical strips of different widths that will then be seamed together. Think of the samples and strips of gingham as units of a composition to be arranged in a pleasing patchwork of various textures, colors, shapes, values, and sizes. It's a challenging compositional problem and a fascinating one. Take plenty of time, mentally planning and actually arranging and rearranging the units of your composition. Again, nothing is final at this stage; you can still move, change, and rearrange at will.

EMBELLISHING THE JOININGS

Begin to study the possibilities of the gingham; try to imagine different ways in which the pattern of the fabric may be changed, enriched, and enhanced. Since it is a symmetrical, repeating pattern, take advantage of this and make it even more so. For instance, stitch horizontal or vertical tucks at regular intervals. Notice what happens to the pattern of checks. How does the predominant color change? How does the value of the piece change? How can this "new" material be used to good advantage as a joining strip between two samples?

Following are a few ways to enhance, change, and vary checked gingham. Experiment with them and add more of

73. *The checked pattern of the gingham emphasized by stitching with a double needle.*

74. *Checks with satin-stitched edges. The dark squares are where checks were cut out, allowing contrasting fabric to show from underneath.*

75. *Quilted and padded squares of gingham alternating with circles of whip stitch.*

your own invention. Use pieces of gingham 3 or 4 inches wider than your widest sample, and from 5 to 6 inches long; these sizes will change with manipulation.

Note that the first of these variation methods involves use of the double needle, a useful tool for the machine embroiderer. Most machines accept the double needle, but you'll have to check your owner's manual or ask your sewing-machine dealer to learn which kind is right for you. Double needles vary according to the type and age of the machine—one make of machine actually accepts two needles in the shank socket, but most use a fork-type needle with a single shank dividing into two needles.

A. Using a double needle and contrasting colors of thread, stitch along the edges of the checks both vertically and horizontally. Try variations of this with different spacings. Use the embroidery foot, teeth, no hoop, and settings for normal dressmaking stitching (straight stitch, average stitch length).

B. Examine the reverse side of what you just did and notice how the under side of the double-needle stitching compares with the right side. You could probably use this to enrich the gingham pattern; experiment on a second joining strip.

C. Create a plaid by combining rows of satin-stitched lines with the check. Use an embroidery foot, teeth, and no hoop; set the stitch width at 2 to 4. See page 38 for satin-stitch setting with teeth and presser foot.

D. Satin stitch on the horizontal and vertical edges of checks. Cut out some of these squares and back them with contrasting fabric. Use the embroidery foot, teeth, no hoop, and the satin-stitch setting. The cut edges might have to be restitched after cutting.

E. Pad and back a piece of gingham, frame it up for free embroidery, and, using straight stitch, no teeth or foot, quilt patterns inside the squares of the check.

F. Embroider small apples in some of the squares, creating a repetitive pattern. Use the hoop, no teeth.

G. Work a pattern of machined buttonholes (consult your owner's manual) on the checks. Thread contrasting ribbon through the buttonholes.

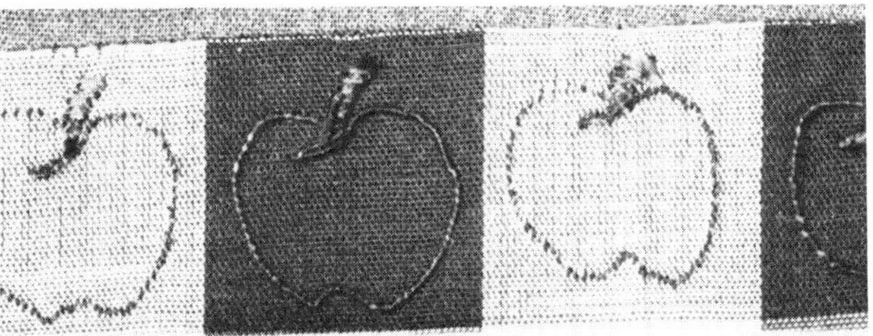

76. *Apple motif repeated in free machining.*

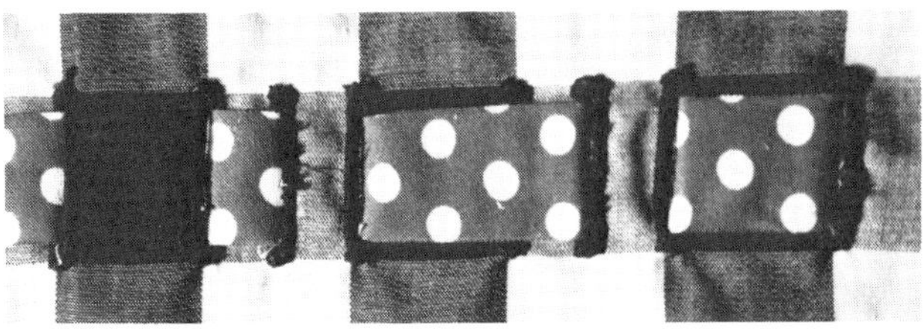

77. *Repeat pattern created by working buttonholes on checked gingham, cutting the holes open, and threading with polka-dot ribbon.*

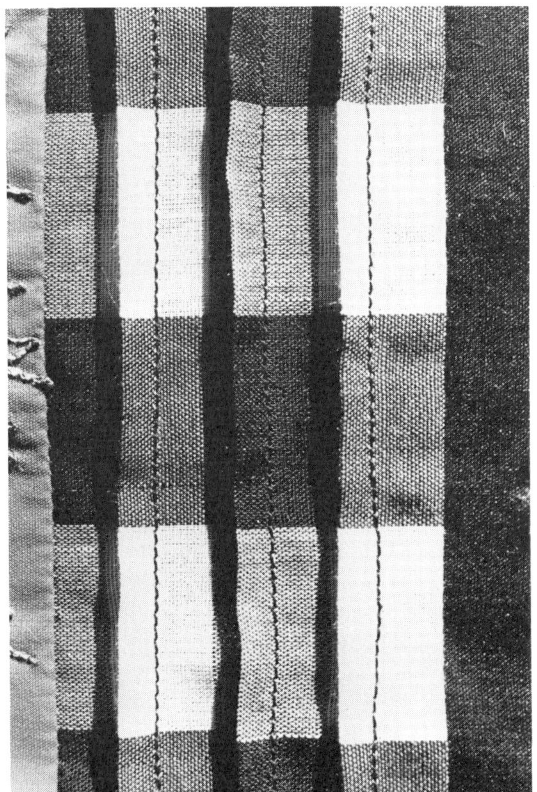

78. *Tucks worked on checked gingham. Note pattern change in area and value.*

H. Create a newly patterned fabric by cutting apart the rows of gingham check, staggering the pattern at new intervals, and seaming the rows together. This can be done vertically, horizontally, and on the bias. Use the presser foot, teeth, and settings for normal stitching.

I. Stitch a series of tucks ½ inch deep following a line of checks of the gingham. Then manipulate these tucks by stitching first in one direction, then in the opposite, at right angles to the tucks (figure 79). Use the presser foot, teeth, and settings for normal stitching.

J. If your machine has automatic cam stitches make combinations of patterned automatic stitches and checks, achieving an entirely new fabric design. A piece of paper under the closely worked stitches will prevent puckers. A similar design can be done by free machining in the hoop, without a foot or teeth (see figure 89). No paper backing is needed for this.

K. Using automatic cam stitches, create a pattern with rows of stitching combined with rickrack and the checks.

L. Make patterns similar to those in J. and K. but using the double needle. When using the double needle for zigzag, experiment to see just how wide a swing is possible before the needle strikes the foot or sole plate. Limit the width of zigzag accordingly, or the needle will break.

ASSEMBLING

As you work with these checked joinings, begin to form vertical strips by stitching together samples and joinings, right sides together, with ½-inch seams. Apply any circular samples to squares or rectangles before joining. Press each seam open as soon as it is stitched. This is especially important because many seams are involved. Using the pattern of checks as a ruler, trim any uneven edges off the samples. Add or subtract fabric where necessary to create a vertical strip of the required length and width (width being determined by the widest sample in the strip—see figure 72). Work for a pleasing relationship between positive and negative areas. Remember, joinings can be cut apart and

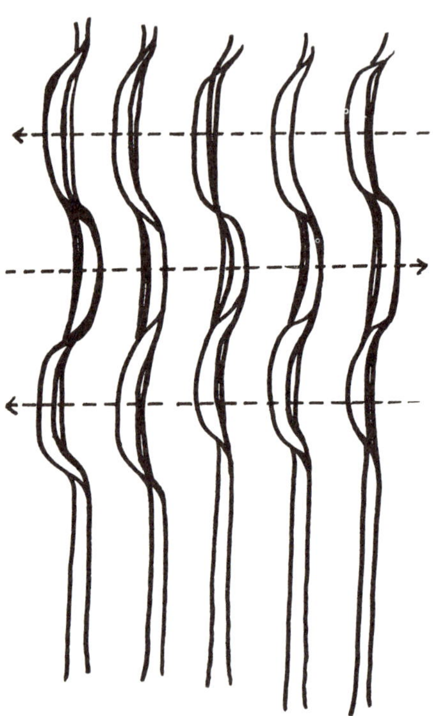

79. *Manipulated tucks.*

reseamed at any time to create the best possible relationship. At this stage the entire piece is still flexible and subject to rearrangement. Do take full advantage of this flexibility.

Form two or three more vertical strips in this fashion, making them the same length as the first, but of different widths. Press open the seams and spread the strips out on the floor to study composition, balance of color, value, line, and area. If any further change is necessary, *now* is the time to do it. When you are completely satisfied with the layout, seam the vertical strips together and press the seams open.

FINISHING

Place the sampler face down on a padded surface and press the entire piece lightly. Trim any uneven seams or edges. Cut a back the same length as the front and 3 inches wider on each side. Press under ½ inch of fabric on the sides of the back. Pin the back to the front (wrong sides facing), centering the front on the back, according to the check pattern. Turn the excess backing fabric to the front, again following the check pattern. This will give you about a 1¼-inch margin of gingham on either side of the front. Press; then top stitch the gingham sides to the front (figure 80).

Finish the top and bottom with open channels to allow wooden dowels or slats to be run through for hanging. Make the channels from your reserved gingham (the top piece is the one 5 inches high, the bottom one, 7), both 2 inches wider than the sampler. Press under ½ inch on one long edge of each strip, and 1 inch on both ends of each strip. Right sides together, centers matching, seam the unturned edge of the 7-inch strip to the back of the sampler bottom, the other one to the back of the sampler top. Press the two seams away from the body of the piece, then fold the strips forward to cover these seams and top stitch the turned edges of the gingham to the sampler front, top and bottom, leaving the turned-under ends open. Now you have a 2-inch channel on the top, a 3-inch one on the bottom (figure 81). Press the

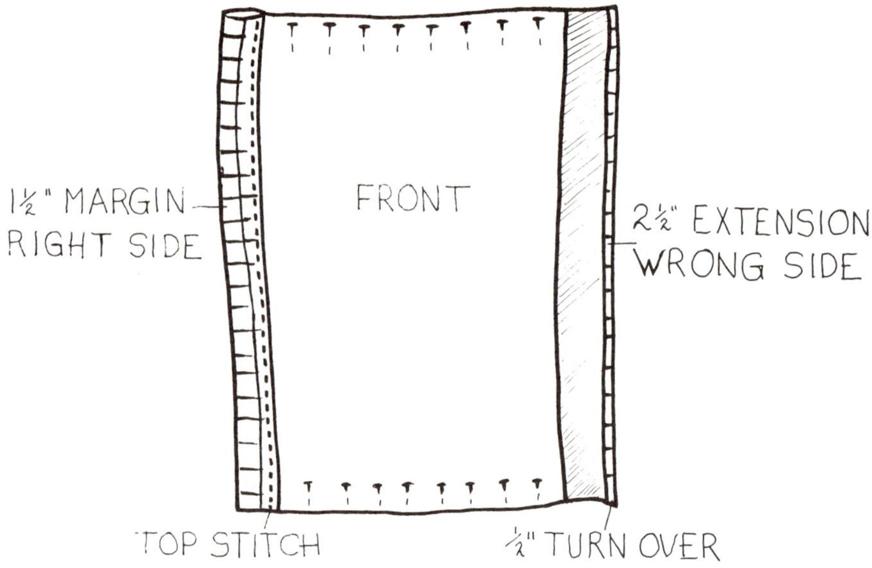

80. *Finishing the sides of the sampler.*

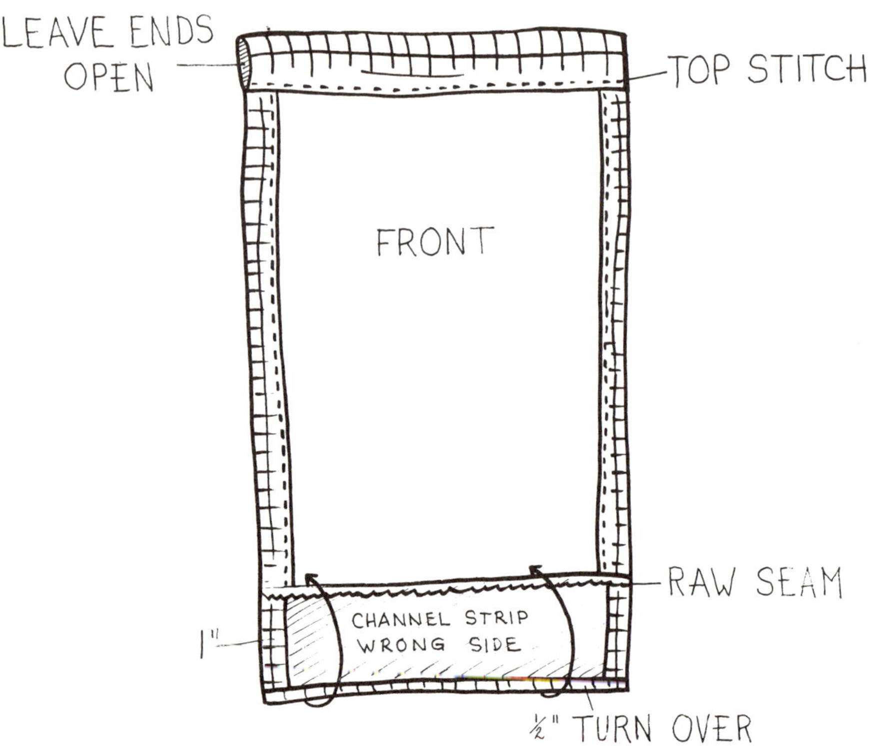

81. *Finishing the top and bottom of the sampler.*

channels, then run a dowel or wooden lath through each—
the bottom lath is necessary because it adds weight. Fasten
screw eyes through the backing into the top lath for easy
hanging. *Voila!* Finished sampler, finished composition,
finished wall hanging. Cheers for the machine embroiderer!

IN CONCLUSION

This is only the beginning. In following the instructions
and working the exercises, you've learned the basics of
machine embroidery and, I hope, discovered first and
foremost that there is no *one* way to use your machine,
which is a wonderfully versatile tool. You've used a variety
of threads and fabrics; used several different feet or none at
all; worked with and without a hoop; used single needles and
double needles and a variety of tensions and settings; and
learned to move fabric in various directions to take full
advantage of the speed of the machine. You've discovered,
in other words, that—as in hand embroidery—a large
number of variations can be given to a basic stitch. In the
next section of the book you'll be building on your
techniques and experimenting. Meanwhile, explore the
myriad possibilities of the techniques you now know.

Study your sampler, too: the nuances of line, texture, and
area that you've already stitched, and imagine other ways of
using them. Whip stitch is lovely for brambly plant stems;
try the double needle for free embroidered rough tree bark;
use cable stitching to add emphasis and contrast to areas of
satin stitch; and remember that nylon hose works beautifully for holding down unwieldy objects such as stones and
shells. Each time you use a stitch analyze its characteristics
and try to envision four or five different ways of using it.

Most of all, enjoy your new art and all the exciting,
beautiful things you can do with it.

82. *Abstract design worked in stitches you're now familiar with: knots, blobs, and cable stitches, with carpet warp used in the bobbin.*

Part Two

PERSONAL WAYS TO USE
AND EXPAND YOUR SKILLS

Totes and More

A stitch or a technique is only that until you use it creatively; then it becomes your own imaginative, personal expression. To get you started in this direction, let's explore some possible projects for using your new-found skills. In this section and the next ones, I'm offering some ideas to get you on your way, but that's all they are—ideas, take-off points for you to start from. Along with these ideas are additional techniques; new skills based on what you've already learned.

I've never known an embroiderer who has enough tote bags for carrying and storing all those threads, fabrics, sewing tools, books, and extra nylons that are standard equipment for supporting the habit. I am certainly no exception. As a result, I've developed a series of simple bags not only to fulfill this obvious need but to explore at the same time the possibilities of machining.

THE BASIC TOTE BAG

Pattern

The basic pattern for the tote bag is a simple one: two rectangular pieces of fabric joined on three sides with welting, a lining, and an attached strap. The strap can be either shoulder length or hand length. The dimensions given in the diagrams are those of my own bags; you may want to

83. A machine-embroiderer's tote bag: a necessity for carrying equipment and a handsome way to show off your skill.

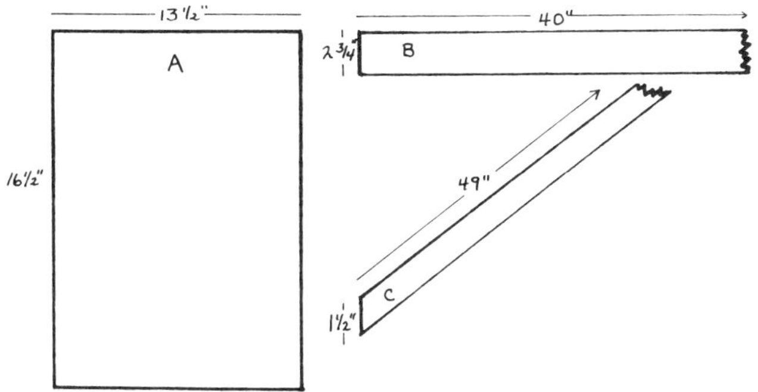

84. Tote-bag pattern. A. Front and back. Use this for two lining pieces as well. B. Strap and lining for strap. C. Welting, cut on the bias.

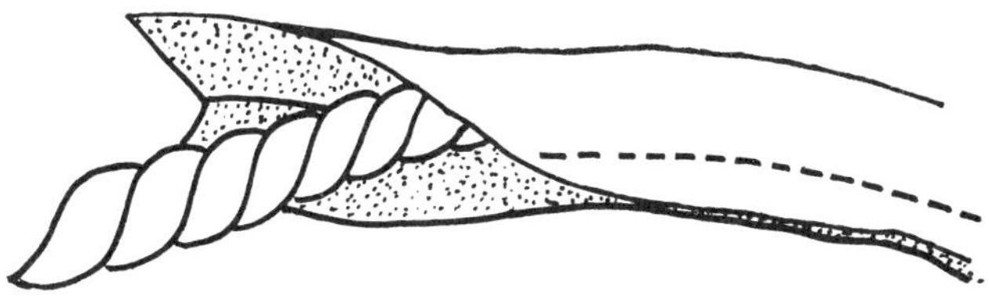

85. Covering cord with bias-cut fabric to form welting.

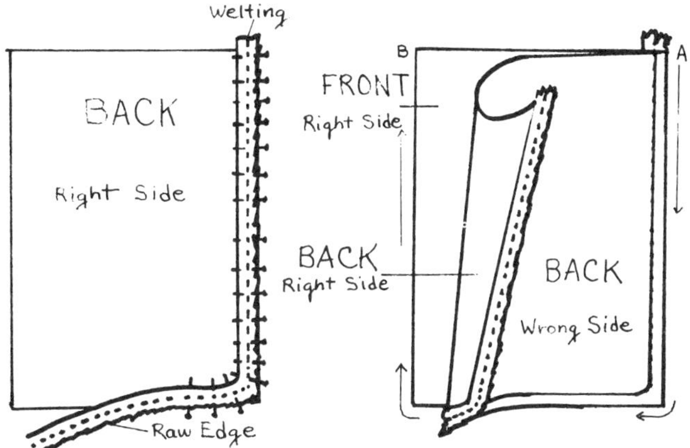

86. Construction of the tote bag.

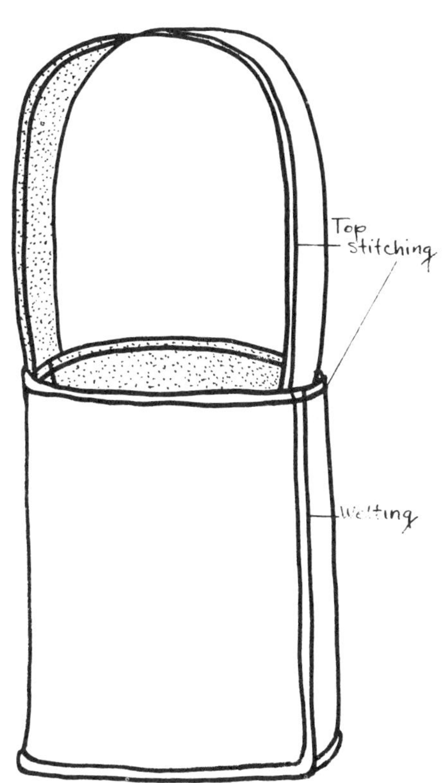

87. Finished tote bag.

change the dimensions to suit your own particular needs and the weight of the materials used.

Construction

I like to use welting on a bag because it gives a tailored, finished appearance. Welting—cord covered by fabric which is then stitched into a seam—can be purchased in upholstery or drapery-fabric shops. To make welting, cut a strip on the bias of the covering material 1½ inches wide and 3 inches longer than the distance around the sides and bottom of your bag. Fold this strip over cord or heavy rug yarn and stitch with the zipper foot.

Pin the welting to the right side of the back of the bag, raw edges matching (figure 86), and allow a bit of extra fullness at the corners to avoid puckering. Stitch with the zipper foot.

Right sides together, pin the front of the bag to the back, matching the corners, and stitch with the zipper foot *just inside* the line of welting stitching (from A to B in figure 86). Turn the bag right side out, and press. Make a lining as you made the bag, but without welting, and use the regular presser foot. Do not turn the lining to the right side.

Cut a strap of the desired length, allowing 1 inch extra at each end for inserting into the bag, and cut lining fabric to match. Press under ¼ inch on the long sides of both the strap and the strap lining. With the wrong sides together, pin the two pieces into place and top stitch together.

Turn down ½ inch on the top of the bag and slip the lining into the bag, pinning bottom to bottom and side to side in the proper position. Press the top edge of the lining toward the wrong side, making it either flush with the top of the bag or allowing a contrasting edge to show. Slip the ends of the strap into position between the top of the lining and the top of the bag. Shoulder straps are centered above the side seams; hand-held straps look better when centered in the middle of the front and back of the bag. Pin or baste the strap in place and top stitch around the entire top of the bag.

88. Geometric designs of free embroidery inside a grid formed of double-needle stitching.

Connecting plastic or metal rings (from hobby and craft shops) and/or cloth loops can be used between the bag and the strap.

DENIM BAG

The blue denim bag in figure C3 was made from some of my son's worn-out jeans, with the faded sections carefully worked into the overall texture of the piece. The red-and-white calico lining, which was also used for the welting, was a remainder from a quilt. The embroidery itself is extremely simple yet effective and fun to do. It's based on the technique you used in exercise A, page 52, when you used a double needle with contrasting colors of thread. I used red on the faded blue denim to form a grid of 2-inch squares (figure 88) like the check of the gingham. Then, in selected squares work free-embroidered motifs (next page) of blobs, circles, and lines. The effectiveness of the design will be dependent on the placement of the blobs, which form the strongest areas of color in your stitching. The blobs will be most effective if they relate to the color of the lining. This color relationship is an important unifying element, relating the stitching to the negative areas of fabric as well as providing an interesting variety of pattern. The individual motifs have infinite variety.

I've found this to be a valuable traveling tote. It has accompanied me back and forth to England many times, since it is lightweight and folds flat for packing. Not only does it hold the necessary London bus and tube map, street guide, wallet, passport case, and small souvenirs, but a camera hanging from my shoulder nestles easily into the top, protecting both the camera and the contents of the bag. Furthermore, the well-worn denim is impervious to the vicissitudes of foreign laundromats.

STRIPED BAG

This second tote can be made from almost any durable fabric, and each fabric could inspire a different type of

89. Free-machined stitching on grey-and-white pillow ticking.

machine embroidery. Grey-and-white striped pillow ticking would be splendid. Preshrink the fabric, of course, then work a variety of linear embroidery on the stripes, either working freely with a hoop or, if your machine has them, using automatic cams (see page 54, J). This is a particularly satisfying way to use the automatic stitches. Whatever your stitch, experiment with different stitch lengths and widths, and combine different colors and values of thread. A variety of linear patterns, combined with the stripe of the fabric and perhaps bits of braid, patterned tapes, heavier couched threads (see Lesson 5), and rickrack create an entirely new fabric. If you plan to give your bag the hard wear and repeated washings I give my denim tote, be sure your fabrics and threads are strong and washable as well as preshrunk.

HIT-AND-MISS PATCHWORK BAG

Patchwork is one of the simplest and most satisfying techniques for combining stitching and fabrics. I know I'm stretching a point in calling certain types of patchwork embroidery when no actual stitching shows on the surface, but patchwork is a particularly good way to combine value, color, and pattern in a single composition without becoming too involved with complicated stitching. So I am choosing to consider patchwork embroidery.

Hit-and-miss patchwork is based on the same process you used to join the samples in your A is for Apple Sampler. Join strips of color- and/or pattern-related fabrics and cut, turn, and rejoin them to make as simple or complex patchwork as you desire. Patchwork is not as durable as a single unseamed piece of cloth, but it makes a striking and unusual accent piece, as well as a handy tote bag.

It is difficult to estimate how much fabric is necessary for hit-and-miss patchwork but I can definitely say that a good deal is required, as each seam reduces the length or width of the strip. Count on losing an inch of fabric with each seam. This is a good way to use up your scrap bag. And I've been amazed what strange colors and patterns somehow blend

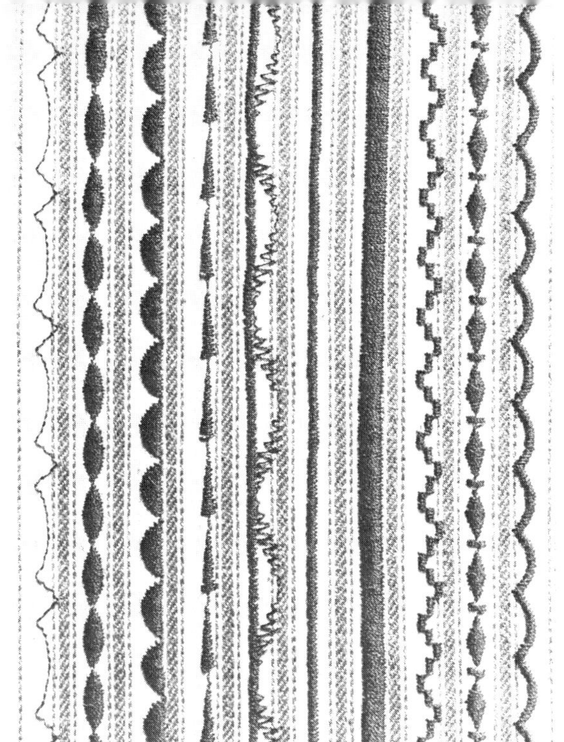

90. *Patterns made by cam stitching on ticking.*

91. *Cam stitching done with a double needle. Stitch length and width were varied to change the pattern.*

92. *Detail of hit-and-miss tartan patchwork. In this case pieces were overlapped and top stitched, using the presser foot and teeth with zigzag set at 4, stitch length at 2.*

93. *Hit-and-miss patchwork showing, left to right, a strip of joined patches, the vertical cut, and the narrower strip reversed top to bottom and seamed to the wider strip.*

effectively in this sort of patching. For this project forget your preconceived notions of color combinations and let your scrap bag explode all over the place. I do suggest you pay some heed to distribution of values, however—don't end up with all the dark patches in one place and the lights in another (unless, of course, your design is built upon such a distribution)—but see that they are distributed in a pleasing, varied pattern of lights and darks. Select fabrics of similar weight and quality. I have successfully combined firmly woven stretch fabric with nonstretch, but it's necessary to choose fabrics of similar weight. I would, for example, avoid using lightweight, gauzy fabric with a woolen tweed or with a nubby, textured drapery fabric. If you simply must use a very thin fabric with a heavier one, use it doubled. But avoid very heavily textured fabrics; they are simply too bulky for the many seams necessary for this type of piecing.

The pieces of fabric may be torn or cut, depending upon the type. Tear if there will not be much raveling or distortion; otherwise, carefully measure and cut the pieces and press them. I find that one of those cutting boards available in fabric shops is invaluable for this. The board unfolds to form a firm cutting surface the size of a double bed and is ruled off in a 1-inch grid, which is a great help in cutting patchwork pieces. Cutting should be either with the vertical or horizontal grain of the fabric; don't use bias cuts.

Step 1. Begin by cutting or tearing pieces of cloth 8 inches wide and from 4 to 10 inches long.

Step 2. Join these pieces, right sides together, allowing a ½-inch seam, arranging a pleasing distribution of colors and values. This is random, so don't try to plan too carefully—it spoils the fun. You'll have a strip of patches 8 inches wide and about 20 inches long (see A, figure 93).

Step 3. Very carefully press all seams in a downward position, rather than open, so they lie in the same direction the presser foot takes in seaming. This type of seam is stronger than one that has been opened and pressed flat. Trim off any unevenness along the edges (the ruled cutting board will aid in this). Cut this strip of patches from top to

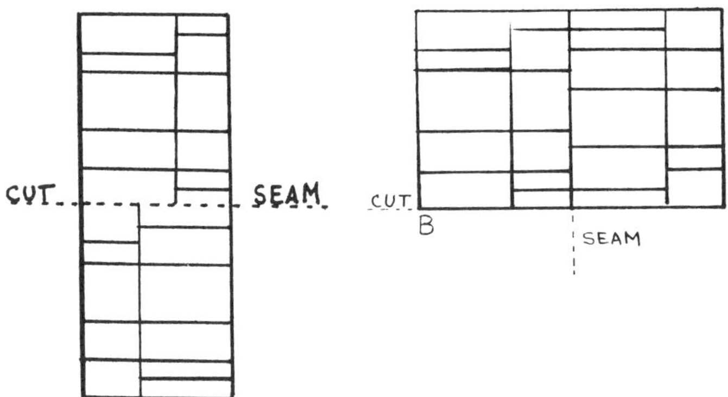

94. *Hit-and-miss patchwork showing variations of the finished piece in preceding figure. A. Finished piece was cut horizontally, the bottom half reversed and stitched to the bottom of the top piece. B. The finished piece, again cut horizontally, with the two halves stitched together at the sides.*

bottom, forming two unequal strips, one 5 inches wide, one 3 (B, figure 93).

Step 4. Reverse the 3-inch-wide strip from top to bottom and press all seams downward. Seam the 3-inch strip vertically to the 5-inch strip (C, figure 93). Observe the completely different pattern effect.

This is the basic procedure for hit-and-miss patchwork, and it can go many directions from this point. The simplest thing to do now is to make a series of strips like the one you have just completed, but using varying widths within it. Examples: a 10-inch-wide strip cut into three strips, 3, 4, and 3 inches wide, with the 4-inch strip reversed. Or, if your fabric is not too heavy, a smaller-scaled strip 6 inches wide, cut into two strips of 2 and 4 inches, or even two 3-inch strips. You'll want to experiment with different proportions and combinations of widths before seaming them together.

To further change the pattern, once you have cut the basic strip and reseamed it vertically, you can fold it in half from top to bottom and make a horizontal cut (figure 94). One of

95. *Skirt of corduroy hit-and-miss patchwork. Model, here and throughout, is Aleta Arthur.*

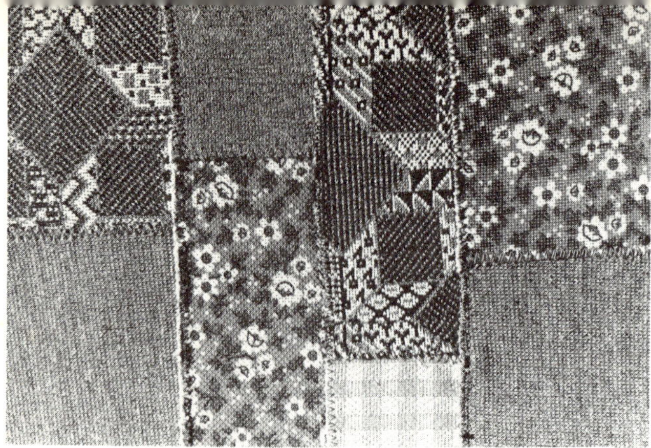

96. *Detail of skirt in figure at right.*

99. *Hit-and-miss-patchwork skirt of doubleknit fabrics.*

97. *Detail of corduroy hit-and-miss-patchwork skirt (preceding page). Attractiveness of the design depends not only on value distribution but on the various directions of the wale.*

98. *Back of the white tote: free-machined doodle quilting.*

100. *Detail of white monochromatic tote showing doodle quilting, manipulated tucks, whip stitch, and needle lace.*

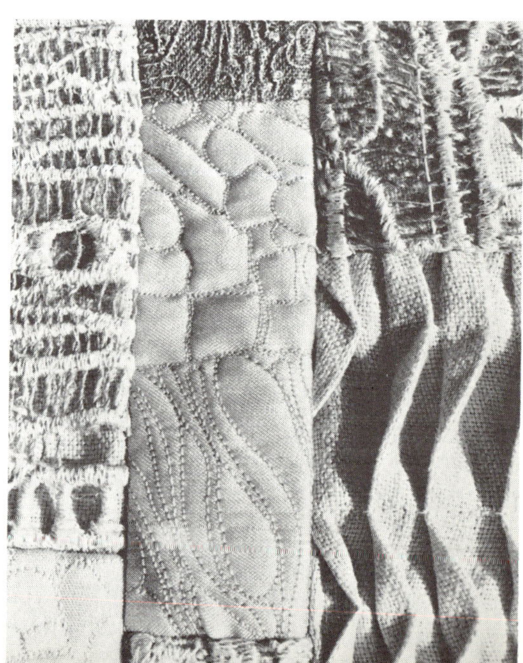

these pieces can be reversed and seamed to the bottom of the other, or reversed and seamed to the side of the other. Again, completely different pattern effects result. Depending upon the size of the original pieces, this process can be continued both vertically and/or horizontally until you reach the desired scale and pattern for your patchwork. And the nice thing is, nothing is final. If, after much cutting and reseaming, you find you do not have a large enough piece for the front and back of your tote you can always make another strip and work it in.

The directions I've given here sound much more complex than they really are. Once you've manipulated a couple of strips you'll find the process is fun and easy, yet the results look tremendously difficult!

Other Patchwork Projects

There are many possibilities for using this sort of patchwork other than for a tote bag. A pillow is even easier—just a tote without lining and strap, with stuffing and, if you wish, a zipper set into a seam. Make enough patchwork yardage for a vest, or use pieces of patchwork to highlight a favorite dress (figure 124). Or how about a heating-pad cover for your pet's basket? I'm saving my husband's elbow- and collar-worn shirts (lovely soft pastels, stripes, and checks) to make a quilt for our first grandchild. The ideas are as much fun as the doing!

I have a fawn-colored skirt made with the same method from old corduroy trousers. The soft, often-washed corduroy looks a good deal like elegant suede, yet presents no cleaning problem. For another patchwork skirt, instead of seaming the pieces together in the ordinary way, I overlapped the fabric edges a scant ½-inch and top stitched with the zigzag set at 4, stitch length at 2½. This skirt, incidentally, is made of all double-knit stretch fabrics and is a delight to pack for traveling. Since it was made of scraps from a number of pants suits, I've at least three tops and several jackets that match some of the pieces in the skirt—a mix-and-match addict's dream!

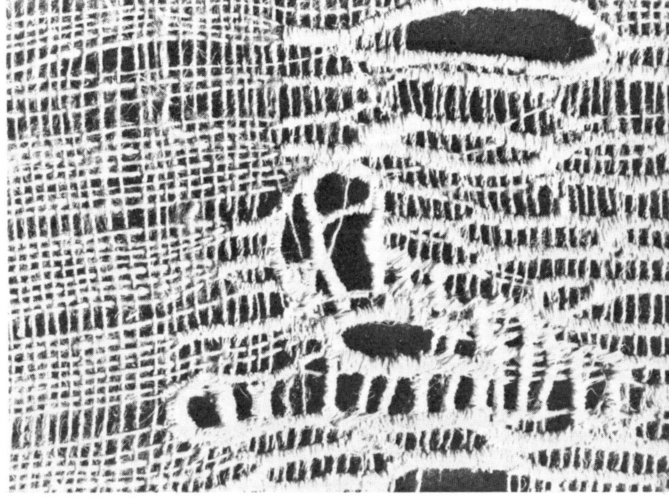

101. Needle lace worked on loosely woven drapery fabric with some warp threads removed.

102. Needle lace worked on burlap with machine-stitched threads added.

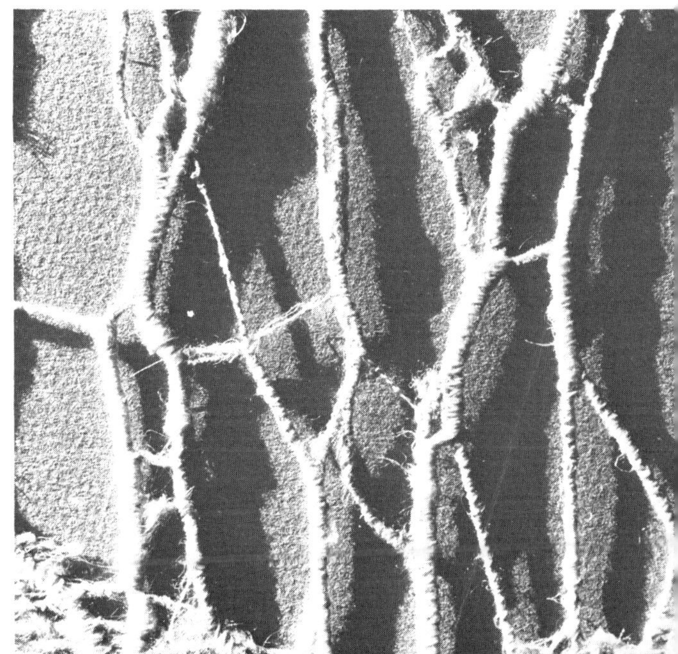

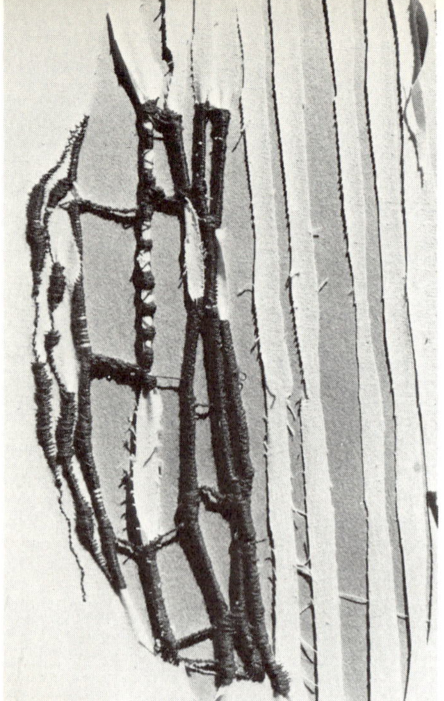

103. *Needle lace worked on slashed fabric, combined with manually adjusted thick-and-thin lines.*

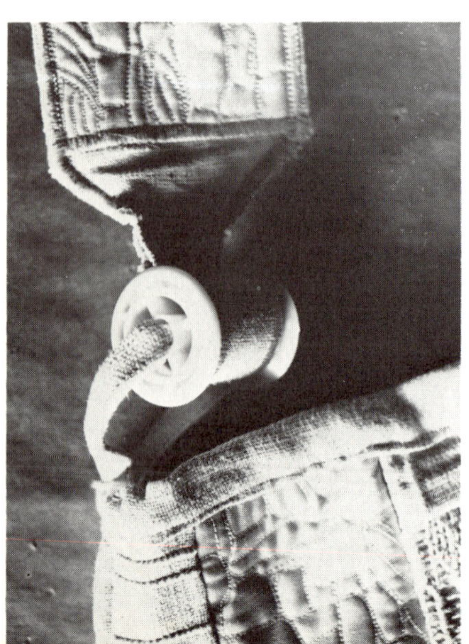

104. *A plastic thread spool serves as a transitional loop between the tote bag and the strap.*

MONOCHROMATIC TOTE

The white tote in figure 83 is really a sampler on the order of the A is for Apple wall hanging, put together with hit-and-miss patchwork. This tote contains a variety of machine techniques that you will recognize from your joinings exercises in Lesson 7, including patterns with the double needle and manipulation of tucks. The tote also includes patterns created with automatic cams as in the pillow-ticking tote earlier in this section; free machining in whip stitch to enhance the tie-dye pattern of the fabric; quilting; and, finally, something new: needle lace.

The free-machined quilting is used in patches on the front of the tote and on the entire back. If you've ever enjoyed doodling with a pencil you'll enjoy this type of quilting. It's done the same way, except with a machine needle on a sandwich of fabric. For the back of the bag use a mediumweight backing fabric—unbleached muslin is good—a thin layer of polyfill quilt batting, and a lightweight fabric for the top. (If the top fabric is too heavy the quilting will not show to best advantage.) I used a semisheer tightly woven dacron curtain fabric. Remember that quilting shows up best on light surfaces—darker fabrics tend to obscure the lovely dark-and-light effect created by the contours of the quilting.

You were introduced to free quilting in Lesson 2, exercise 4, working with three layers of fabrics framed in a hoop. The hoop can become a problem when you're quilting large areas or thick layers of fabrics and batting. In this event, instead of a hoop use the quilting/darning foot, which stabilizes the fabric, but allows you to drop the teeth and move the fabric freely in all directions. (The quilting foot may also be used without a hoop for embroidering on velvets and other piled fabrics that might be permanently marked by a hoop's pressure.)

Pin or hand baste the three layers of material together, working from the center out toward the edges in all directions. Do not stretch the fabric, but keep it smooth and taut. Use straight stitching. (You might like to experiment later with the zigzag stitch for quilting; it's different and interesting.) Begin in the center, and work gradually outward in all directions, doodling with the needle the way you would with a pencil. You'll see that designs are formed through the relationship between (again!) positive and negative areas. Stitching depresses the fabric, sending it into shadow; the unstitched areas, pushed by the polyfill underneath, rise up to catch the light, and the contrast of light and dark is indeed lovely. Free quilting has unlimited design possibilities and would work equally well for a skirt, cushion, vest, or even a long evening cape. Have fun with it!

New Technique: Needle Lace

Needle lace is done on *very* loosely woven fabric. I look for remnants of drapery fabrics (see figure 101). You should be able to withdraw individual threads easily, as well as push and manipulate the remaining ones. A slightly different effect may be achieved by cutting slits in tightly woven fabric and working in the same manipulating fashion, as in figure 103. In both cases take care to keep the fabric taut, but especially in the second case, as the cut fabric will move and vibrate more than the manipulated threads will.

To make needle lace, frame your fabric in a hoop, drop or cover the teeth, and set your machine for a wide zigzag. The object of this is to clump the threads of the fabric with the zigzag, creating a pattern of open, lacelike areas. Try it, feeling the threads moving and bunching beneath the swinging needle. You'll find the number of threads changes as the fabric moves—that's fine. The result should be a constantly changing pattern. As you become accustomed to this technique you'll find it's possible to shape and direct the threads horizontally as well as vertically. Some of the withdrawn threads can be worked back in, creating heavier textures in places. Stitching can be taken across open spaces, then reinforced with zigzag. This is an extremely mobile, versatile type of embroidery, with many possible uses. In the tote, small samples of needle lace are used as patches in the patchwork; later we'll see it used for clothing.

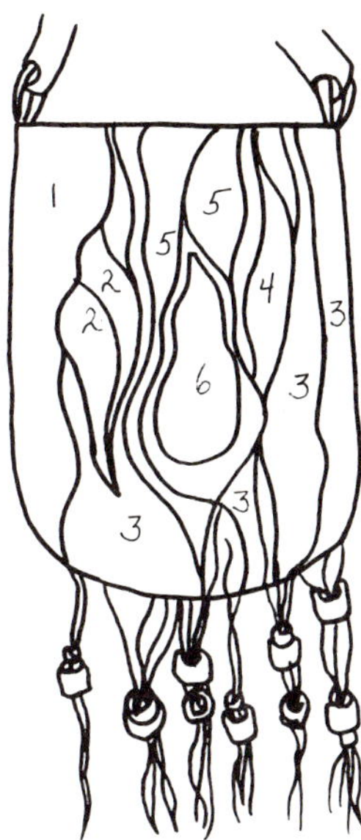

105. *Diagram of areas of the shag bag.*

106. *Satin stitch (Gobelin) on canvas.*

107. Detail of shag bag showing satin stitching on canvas. Holes cut in the canvas allow the dark lining to show through.

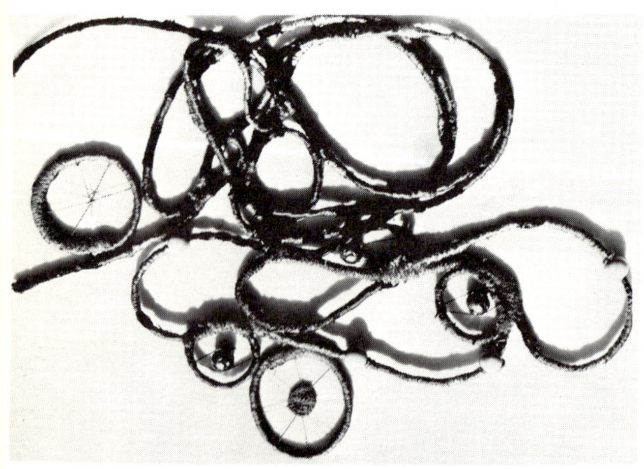

108. Wrapped cords, some strung with wooden beads, that have been manipulated into a variety of curves and circles. The beads inside the circles were applied by hand; the spiderwebs were worked by machine.

One feature of this bag that all embroiderers will appreciate is the use not of plastic rings to connect the strap to the bag, but instead, empty thread spools. The ivory-colored plastic spools have a decorative openwork at each end which relates nicely to the open lacework of the stitching; they harmonize in color and make a good transition between the loops of the bag and the shoulder-length strap.

SHAG BAG

The blue-and-tan shag bag (figure C10) involves some of the techniques you have done before and introduces two new ones. The bag is worked on a very loosely woven linen drapery fabric, the kind that lends itself nicely to manipulation and change. Actually, here you will be creating almost a new fabric through a combination of threads and stitchery. Area 2, figure 105 is similar to the padded areas in exercise 23, in which you made a three-dimensional collage of the half-apple. In the present case, polyfill has been tucked under a free-form shape of nylon hose and held in place by a few lines of quilting, which serve not only to hold the fabric in place but add considerably to the curvilinear motion throughout the bag. This is an example of contoured, three-dimensional appliqué applied from the front.

Area 3 involves the type of couching you did for your wall panel in exercise E, page 36, when you looped heavy yarn over your finger or a pencil before couching. Here, rug yarns and ravelings from the ground fabric are looped for couching. Some of the loops are clipped, others left as loops. You will notice that a variety of colors are combined in this way, forming a heavy, multicolored shag that ultimately resolves itself into a beaded, knotted fringe made from uneven strands of the same types of threads dripping from the bag. Area 4 is a section of the ground fabric embroidered with the needle lace described earlier. The open spaces allow the dark brown of the lining to show through, which relates to the dark brown threads used in the shag. Area 5 has a variety of couched threads, which again carry out the downward, undulating motion of the entire piece. Some of the threads are tied with closely spaced knots, giving a beaded texture to the line.

New Techniques

Machined "Needlepoint"

Areas 1 and 6 of figure 105 involve new techniques. Area 6 is a piece of "needlepoint" canvas worked by machine. The stitching here in effect is a machined Gobelin stitch worked in different directions to fill the shape. I used No. 10 canvas and simply satin stitched over different numbers of threads, depending upon the texture I wanted and the swing of the needle. It's a good idea to experiment with needlepoint canvas of different sizes to see just how many threads the various settings will cover. Work without the presser foot for this, and without a hoop—the canvas is stiff enough that no hoop is necessary. This is a quick way to work the stylized Florentine and bargello patterns.

The finished piece of canvas is attached with a few connecting threads, allowing a good deal of the brown lining to show around it. This area works well with the openwork parts of area 4.

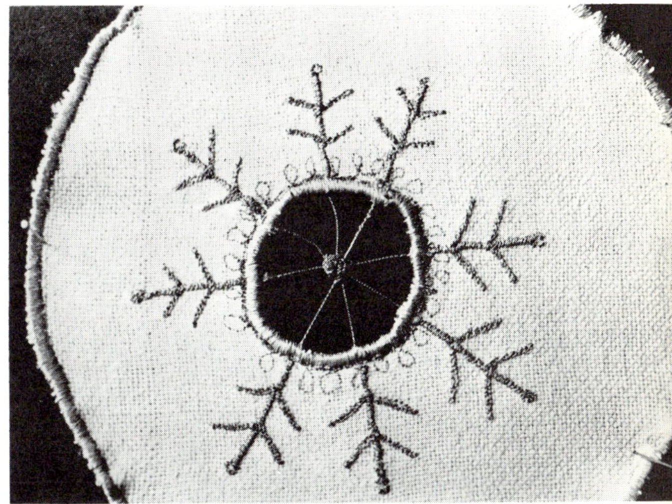

109. *Machined spiderweb in free-machined snowflake motif; straight stitch and zigzag set on 1.*

Wrapped Cord

The second new technique appears in area 1, where a machine-wrapped jute cord is twisted, twined, and couched at intervals to form a strong linear design. You did something quite similar to this in exercise B, page 35, when you covered a jute cord with closely spaced zigzag. But then the cord was attached to fabric—this time only the cord itself is wrapped with stitching.

Set up the machine for free embroidery and drop the teeth, but use the quilting or darning foot, which will serve to stabilize the cord and keep it from jumping out of place as you stitch. Lock the thread securely in the cord by straight stitching up and down several times at the beginning; then switch to No. 4 zigzag and stitch over the cord as you slowly pull it along under the foot. End as you began, by straight stitching in place two or three times. This technique works on any cord no larger in diameter than the maximum swing of the needle.

After you have achieved some proficiency in wrapping the cord evenly, try doubling the cord back on itself at intervals, forming interesting shapes with the coils (figure 108). Fasten intersections by zigzagging in place three or four times to anchor one coil to the other. These wrapped cords can become interesting objects in themselves since they can be twisted and formed into free-standing, three-dimensional pieces and may be further enhanced with beads, spiderwebs (below), and other embellishments.

THE SPIDERWEB

One machine technique as yet unmentioned here, and closely related to openwork needle lace, is the spiderweb. Reminiscent of Ayrshire embroidery, that beautiful hand-embroidered cutwork of the nineteenth century, the spiderweb consists of delicate weblike stitching to fill open areas that have been cut in the fabric and edged with satin stitching. The success of the design depends not only on the delicacy of the filling stitches, but also on the relationship between the fabric and the openwork.

To make machined spiderwebs, you need a fabric that is quite firm, and it must be very tightly framed in the hoop. Tight framing is especially important, because each time a hole is cut in the fabric, the fabric becomes less taut and more apt to vibrate under the needle. Use normal tension top and bottom, and settings for free machining. The spiderweb is stitched in four steps:

Step 1. Using the straight stitch, stitch three or four times in a circle around the area to be cut.

Step 2. Remove the fabric from the hoop, cut out the fabric just inside the stitched circle, and reframe tightly.

Step 3. Supporting the edges of the hole firmly with your fingers, anchor the thread by stitching it in place several

110. The four steps of making a spiderweb.

111. Machined spiderwebs and satin stitching combined in a cutwork flower: white thread on yellow linen.

113. White collar with pendants of machine embroidery on canvas.

112. Detail from the Four Seasons Panel showing machined spiderweb snowflake combined with satin stitch.

114. Detail of the white collar.

115. *When making a collar, choose a pattern that rests properly on your neck.*

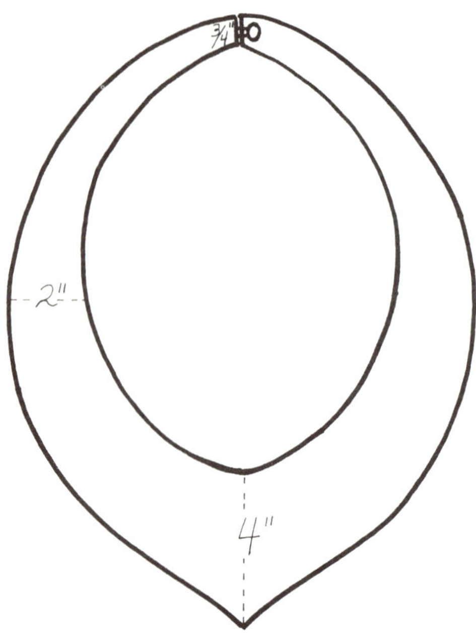

116. *Suggested collar dimensions.*

times on the edge of the hole, then stitch across the open space to the other side, forming the spokes of the web. If the thread has a tendency to break, be sure the tensions are equal top and bottom and that you are supporting the fabric edges firmly. Anchor the thread to the other side as before, then stitch around the hole to the next position and form the next spoke. The spokes can be spaced symmetrically or asymmetrically, according to your design. You might want to stitch a circular motif in the center of the web at the intersection of the threads before coming out to the edge for the last spoke.

Step 4. Finish off the edge with a neat, free-machined satin stitch. Additional free machining may be added at this point—use your imagination to create a stylized snowflake or star, or to extend the web design onto the fabric.

Obviously this is a delicate stitch, subject to snagging and breaking, and therefore not appropriate for anything that would receive hard wear. But for wall hangings, evening bags, and collars, it can be a valuable addition to your machine-embroidery vocabulary.

Figure 111 shows the spiderweb worked in white on yellow linen and combined with white satin stitching in a traditional cutwork treatment. Backed with fabric in a slightly contrasting color, or with linen in another value of yellow, it would work nicely for a crisp, summer evening bag.

Spiderweb with Wrapped Cord

Figure 108 shows the spiderweb combined with wrapped cords and beads. Some of the beads were strung on the jute cord as it was machine wrapped, others were suspended in the coils of the wrapped cord by hand. To make a spiderweb with wrapped cord, first wrap the cord and form it into a circle, securely stitching the ends together; then work the spiderweb according to step 3, page 72. Be sure to support the circle firmly with your fingers as you stitch across the opening, since you have no fabric here. You might also use the quilting or darning foot for added stability. Laced onto a lightweight wooden frame, this variation of the spiderweb could be used for a see-through room-divider panel, providing a delicate linear design that could be enjoyed from either side. You also might work the spiderwebs on organdy or curtain sheer, set the entire piece between sheets of plexiglass, and hang it in a window or French door.

Figure 112 shows the winter detail from a wall panel entitled the Four Seasons. Here spiderwebs are used as the centers of snowflakes, combined with line- and satin-stitched snowflakes. The white spiderwebs, backed with white fabric, result in a textural contrast that adds a great deal to the rich tone-on-tone effect of this section of the panel.

ELEGANT COLLARS

The blue collar (figure C14) is made of strands of wrapped cords and is hung with pendants of machine-embroidered canvas. Clay beads hang in the centers of the pendants.

The white collar (figure 113) combines hand-worked drawn fabric (the neck piece) with machine-embroidered pendants featuring openwork and spiderwebs. The raised stitches and the pearls on the pendants were applied by hand. This collar is a good example of how hand and machine embroidery can be combined in a compatible fashion.

Simple but distinctive embroidered collars can be cut from your favorite round-necked dress pattern. Choose a pattern that fits well and rests where you want it to. The Egyptian Collar and the End of the Rainbow Collar, both made from a dress pattern, are each worked in a combination of waled and encroaching satin stitch on linen. They're backed with the same fabric, and fasten at the back with a button and loop. The coins in the pot with the rainbow are satin stitched in gold metallic thread.

117. *Egyptian Collar.*

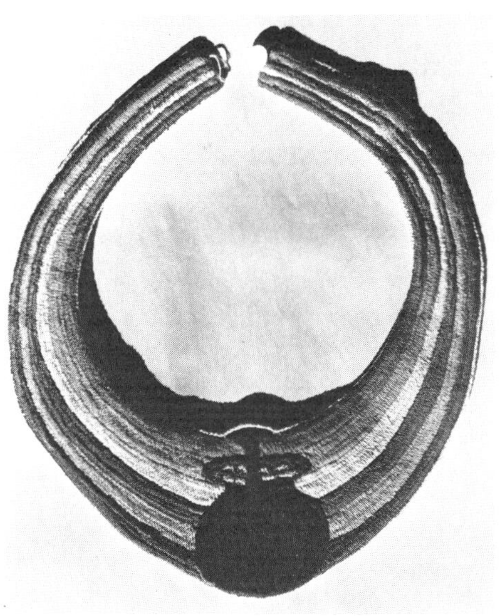

118. *End of the Rainbow Collar.*

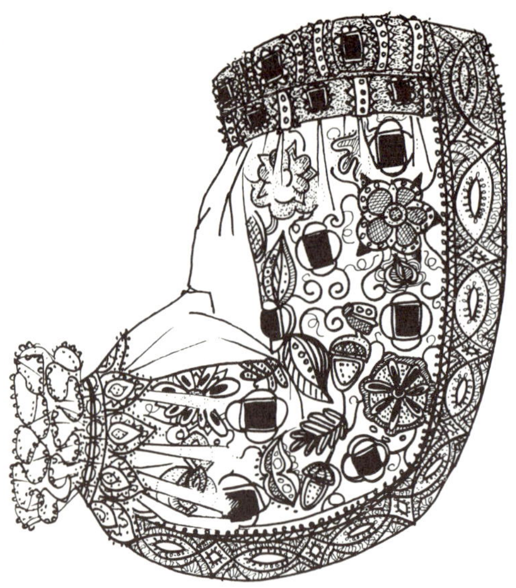

119. *Sleeve of a dress of Elizabeth I, from a Gheerardt portrait in Hever Castle, Kent. The sleeve is embroidered in black and enriched with gold threads and multicolored jewels set in gold. Intricately worked gold lace extends in a band down from the center of the sleeve from shoulder to wrist. At the shoulder is a heavy strip of black velvet with insets of multicolored stones, pearls, and gold lace. A transparent, very full puffed sleeve covers the entire blackwork one, ending at the wrist in a needlepoint lace cuff bordered in gold.*

120. *Seminole patchwork.*

Art You Can Wear

Decoration of clothing is probably one of the oldest uses of embroidery. Unfortunately, fabrics are less durable than stone, so we know of the earliest forms of embroidery indirectly—through early sculpture and excavated artifacts. Prehistoric people threaded thorn and bone needles with plant fibers and animal sinews to stitch together animal skins; whether anyone embellished the final garments is not known. We do know, however, that the ancient Chinese were probably the first people to use quilting, which provided warmth and protection in battle, as well as ornamentation; and the Copts, the early Christians in Egypt, are remembered for the beautiful stylized bands of embroidery worked into their woven garments.

History records little of what was spoken in 1520 at the meeting between Henry VIII of England and Francis I of France on the Field of Cloth of Gold, but we do have an impressive description of fabrics with warps of gold wire glittering in the sunshine and of the garments of the two rulers—so heavily embroidered with metal threads and precious stones that movement was impeded. We know, too, that embroidered garments at that meeting were not restricted to people; the horse that Francis rode wore a mantle of blue-and-gold fabric that was embellished with an embroidered pattern of fleur de lis.

Queen Elizabeth I was her father's daughter in many

ways, and her wardrobe was one of them. Paintings of her show fantastic collars of needle lace, slashed sleeves that allowed rich underfabrics to be pulled through, embroidered ribbons and stomachers, skirts heavy with metal threads, petticoats with intricate crewelwork, and beautifully embroidered gloves and shoes of white kid.

On our own continent, Indian quillwork in beautifully stylized patterns on shirts, bags, and moccasins, and Seminole patchwork certainly were and are as colorful and dramatic in their own way as Henry's cloth of gold was. And I shall never forget an Eskimo shirt I once saw, glowing with a soft, moon-glow irridescence, and completely covered with appliqué of fish scales!

SPECIAL FACTORS IN EMBROIDERY FOR CLOTHES

Compositional problems in clothing embroidery are similar to those of other forms of embroidery—you should still strive for unity, interest, and variety, and for a pleasing relationship between positive and negative areas. But clothing embroidery presents additional problems. Because garments are intended to be worn, the personal contours of the wearer must be considered: good features should be emphasized, poorer ones camouflaged. In my own case, my hips are far more ample than I would wish, hence I try to emphasize a long, flowing motion from neck to hem, with emphasis around the bottom of the skirt and no stops or interruptions in the hip region. A heavy-busted woman would do well to center the interest of her embroidery on sleeves or a hem, playing down the upper part of the garment. Quilting is effective around a hem since it adds weight as well as dramatic interest. Remember too that a garment will be seen in motion the greater part of the time—a fascinating problem to consider. In fact, I find this one of the most delightful things about embroidered clothing: each movement of the body changes the pattern and proportion of the embroidered areas, and new designs are constantly being created.

When you're choosing a pattern for a garment intended

121. *Simple patterns of straight stitch—worked with teeth and presser foot, no hoop—relate the collar, sleeves, and hem to constructional elements of this garment. Seams are top stitched, and decorative stitching controls the fullness on sleeves and waist.*

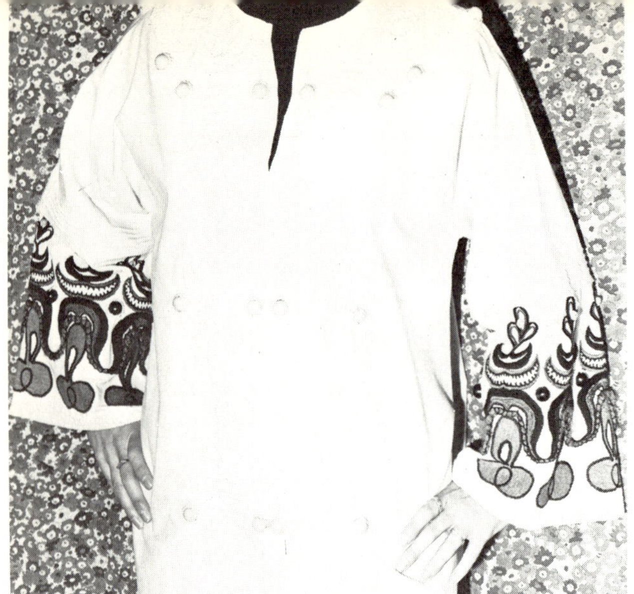

122. *White tunic. The vertical design of the front is used horizontally on the sleeves in a combination of appliqué, free satin stitching, and hand couching. Rows of small tucks serve as transitional elements to relate the stitched areas of the garment to the unstitched areas.*

123. *Detail of the front of the white tunic: white-on-white free-machined satin stitching and blobs. This vertical design, although not identical to the sleeve embroidery, is similar and gives a sense of unity.*

for embroidery, simplicity is the better part of valor. Simple tunics, skirts without pleats or gathers, and the beautiful square-cut ethnic garments are best. With these you avoid complicated darts, gores, and seams that would be distracting to the embroidered composition. One of my favorites is the floor-length caftan—a simple rectangle with an opening for the head. (I'm using the term "caftan" here in the popular sense; the true Middle-Eastern caftan usually has sleeves and a hood.) With the pattern I prefer, the caftan falls in an unbroken line from neck to hem, folds gently as the arms move, and, with a rod passed through both armholes, can be used as a wall hanging as well.

Another important thing to consider in designing embroidery for clothing is relating the embroidery to the design of the garment. We've all seen so-called embroidered garments that have a little spot of stitching on a pocket—often unstrategically situated just at the point of one breast—or a weak little line of stitching on a collar or cuff. This doesn't mean that the entire garment must be covered with stitching; in fact, a few carefully placed, beautifully worked areas of embroidery can be most effective and carry a great deal of impact. But they must be carefully thought out and related in some way to the rest of the garment.

On the subject of fabric, I would advise using washable, preshrunk fabrics whenever possible.

COORDINATING EMBROIDERY WITH THE GARMENT

The white tunic (figure 122) illustrates three successful ways to coordinate embroidery, fabric, and garment design. The design for the embroidery here was developed from cut paper, much like a cut-out chain of paper dolls. If you look closely, you will see that the vertical design worked down the front of the tunic in white machining is the same repetitive motif that is stitched horizontally around the bottom of the sleeve. Although interpreted differently, the two designs are closely related, adding unity to the tunic. In both cases I have allowed a good deal of the white fabric to show through the embroidered design, forming an important negative element in the design. This is one example of relating embroidery to the ground fabric. A second example is the white-on-white, free-machined stitching down the front; it not only forces more attention toward the sleeves, which is what I wanted, but it also relates, through color, to the fabric. A third method is the use of several rows of small tucks on the sleeves, just above the appliqué and couching, a beautifully simple way to relate embroidery to ground fabric. In this case, the fabric has been manipulated and changed through stitching in such a way that both fabric and stitches are involved, thus bridging the gap between plain fabric and solid stitching. Tucking is a subtle and successful transitional mechanism.

The sleeve treatment is a combination of free-machined satin stitching and direct frontal appliqué finished with a hard edge of satin stitching. The heavy thick-and-thin yarn is couched by hand, but it could be as easily couched on the machine. The wooden beads are set in sockets of hand-worked, raised buttonhole stitch.

The Pink Panther Tunic (figure C4), which is made from the same pattern as the white one, was actually a practice piece for satin stitching. Satin stitching requires practice to do easily and well, but I discovered long ago that I don't like to sit down and simply practice; it's much more fun to work on some interesting project that involves the discipline. The Pink Panther Tunic served that end. The design was developed from an illustration in a children's book but changed and stylized to suit the areas of the garment. Notice that even though the lines of satin stitching are fairly closely worked, areas of fabric still show through and become part of the design, and the grey of the fabric becomes an important color in the scheme.

The blue dress (figure 124) is cut from the same uncluttered type of pattern as the tunics, but this time there are set-in sleeves. The yoke, sleeve bands, and the band around the bottom of the skirt are all made of hit-and-miss patchwork, but they are applied to the surface rather than being set in, as true patchwork would be. The patchwork

124. Blue tie-dyed dress enhanced with areas of hit-and-miss patchwork. Bits of blue fabric in the patchwork relate to the ground fabric, and rows of tucks provide a transition between plain and patched areas.

bands are placed in such a way that bands of the blue dress fabric (the negative areas) become part of the design, as do rows of tucks.

CONSTRUCTION CONSIDERATIONS

Cutting Out the Garment

If you're making a garment from a paper pattern, it is best to mark the pattern on the fabric—but *do not cut it out.* There are two reasons for that. First, as you have already discovered, for most machine embroidery it is necessary to frame the fabric in a hoop. And in order to do that, excess fabric is necessary. However, once in a while it is unavoidable that an area intended for embroidery will come so close to the edge of the fabric that it is impossible to frame it. In that case, simply baste another piece of fabric to the edge and remove it when the embroidery has been completed.

The second reason for not cutting out the pattern immediately is that this gives you a chance to spread it all out, much as you did with the samples when you were planning your A is for Apple Sampler. The garment is still at a flexible, changeable stage; if necessary a sleeve can be lengthened to accommodate tucks, or a pocket can be enlarged or made smaller to better suit the nature of your embroidery design. I usually trace around the paper pattern with chalk; it does have to be renewed from time to time if cutting is delayed very long, but it's handy because it can be brushed off and changed easily.

Transferring a Design

The white design and the pink panther were both first drawn on paper and then transferred to fabric. When I do this, I trace my embroidery design with a felt-tip pen on layout paper, which is quite strong, yet transparent enough to allow a felt-pen line to be seen from the wrong side. (You can purchase layout paper at art-supply shops.) Then I redraw my design on the *wrong* side of the layout paper,

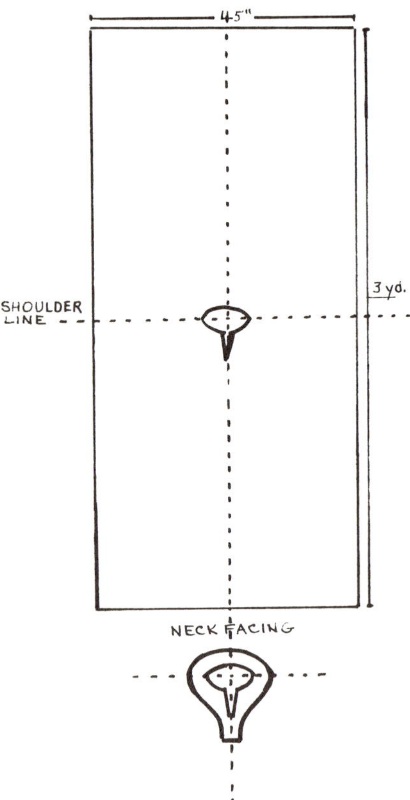

125. *The basic rectangle for a "caftan."*

making a firm, solid line with a commercial transfer pencil. (This is a soft, waxy pencil available in dressmaking and notions shops.) I carefully position my pattern, transfer side down, on the right side of the fabric, and iron over it with a medium-hot iron, being careful not to move the paper pattern while ironing. (It's well to experiment first on scrap fabric with the transfer pencil if you haven't used one before.) The design is now on the fabric, and it can be washed out after the embroidery is finished. If you're doing this and find you've marked a too-heavy line and have trouble washing it out, soak the area for a while in one of the commercial presoaking stain and soil removers (you can see why a washable fabric is desirable here).

SQUARE-CUT GARMENTS

Basic Pattern

The square-cut ethnic garment lends itself beautifully to embroidery and can take many forms. It is timeless in style, never truly in fashion and certainly never out. Thus it is well worth the time and effort given to the embroidery that enriches it. This garment fits all sizes and shapes of people, and it requires very little knowledge of dressmaking for construction. There are three basic types of square-cuts: the rectangle, the rectangle with appendages, and the composite rectangle (nomad dress, figures 133 and C1).

The rectangle is, obviously, the simplest of the three, and needs very little knowledge of dressmaking to construct. I'm including here instructions for a rectangular caftan just to encourage you to think about shape and to provide an easy garment idea to get you embroidering. The measurements given here are for 40- to 45-inch fabric, which results in midarm-length sleeves. Use narrower fabrics for shorter sleeves, wider fabrics for long sleeves. Three yards of fabric (1½ yards each for front and back) allow for a 1½-inch hem and will make a garment for a person 5 feet, 6 inches tall, but the length can easily be adjusted. The shape of the neck can be varied to suit your taste; a round or square opening can be cut, or a variation of your favorite commercial pattern.

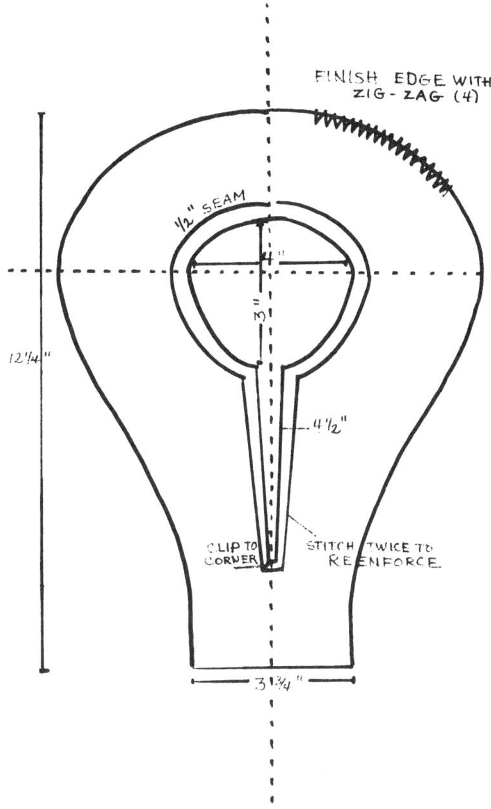

126. Caftan neck facing.

Before planning the embroidery, mark the vertical and horizontal centers of the fabric. (The horizontal center will be the caftan shoulder line, the vertical center will mark the midfront and midback.)

Plan and work your embroidery while the garment is still flat and unseamed; remember that it will most often be seen as a separate front and back. Each should be a well-planned, complete composition, related to the other. After the embroidery has been completed, cut out a neck facing and, rather than hemming it, zigzag around its outside edge, using the presser foot, teeth, and normal dressmaking setting. Mark the vertical and horizontal centers of the facing, then spread the caftan flat on your cutting board, right side up, and pin the neck facing to the caftan (right sides together), matching the vertical and horizontal centers. Straight stitch twice around the seam line of the neck opening, reinforcing the bottom of the point by stitching one or two extra times. Cut out the neck opening, clip the curves to the seam line, and clip the point as shown in figure 126. Turn the facing to the inside and press; then tack the outside edge of the facing to the garment.

On the wrong side of the caftan, starting 7 inches down from the shoulder line, stitch ½-inch side seams. Turn to the right side and press the seams open. Hem the caftan, and press once more to complete.

The Flower-garden Caftan

There are as many ways of embroidering a caftan as there are ideas. If you don't feel ready to start out entirely with your own design, consider applying a wide band of flower-printed fabric to the bottom of a piece of solid-color fabric. Appliqué the band in a slightly uneven line, roughly following the shape of the flower pattern, and stitch with light, widely spaced zigzag set at 4 (figure 127). Then frame up what you've done for free machining, and add some embroidery to some of the flowers in the printed pattern. Cut out individual flowers from the printed fabric and appliqué them above the border, tying them into the

127. Detail of Flower-garden Caftan. A. Printed fabric, cut out and applied. B. Machine embroidery. C. Re-embroidered printed fabric. D. Applied printed fabric. E. Widely spaced zigzag for a soft edge on the appliqué. F. Free-machined stems.

flowered border with embroidered stems and leaves. Embroider some flowers and leaves on the ground fabric. If you find the border of printed fabric around the bottom seems too solid, cut out bits of the printed design, allowing some of the ground fabric to show through, again relating positive to negative areas. The cover of the book shows a detail of a caftan involving these techniques.

"Plant" more flowers down the length of the sleeve or around the cuff, or make an interesting arrangement around the neck opening, or grow one very long-stemmed flower up the front! There are many different ways you can handle this motif, all with ideas taken from the printed fabric. Remember, relate the positive areas to the negatives and work for a pleasing, interesting composition. And when you're not wearing your flower garden, run a wooden dowel through the armholes and display it as a wall hanging.

The Four Seasons Caftan

The Four Seasons Caftan (figure C7) is a simple rectangle with an opening for the head. It represents the seasons of the year and features two large trees extending almost the entire length of the garment. Half of one tree is in spring blossom; a squirrel bounds down the trunk and dandelions grow around the bottom. Summer, the other half of the same tree, shows it fully leafed with a robin on one limb. Wildflowers grow in the lush grass at the base of the tree (figure C9), a raccoon peers around the trunk, and wild strawberries and hedgehogs flourish at the bottom. (I've shown all my favorite flora and fauna.) The reverse side of the caftan, fall and winter, can be worn as the front depending upon season and whim. Here half the other tree suggests fall, with colored leaves changing from green to red and gold. At the base of the trunk goldenrod and Queen Anne's lace add to the autumnal scene, where a squirrel is eating nuts and a chipmunk nibbles on red berries. The winter half shows snow-hung branches and flakes of snow in the air; the snowy ground area is patterned with delicate black-and-white twigs and brambles.

128. Detail from the Four Seasons Caftan: raccoon worked in encroaching satin stitch. Stitching done with a double needle raises up on the tree trunk lines of fabric that give the effect of a rough, barklike texture. This stitching process is sometimes known as pin tucking (see A, page 52).

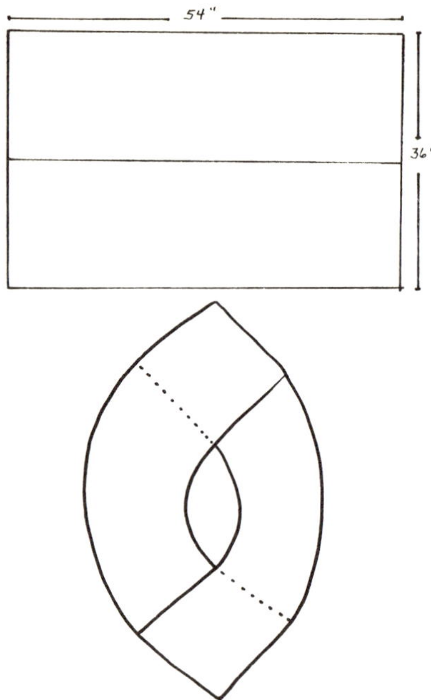

129. *Pattern for triangular poncho.*

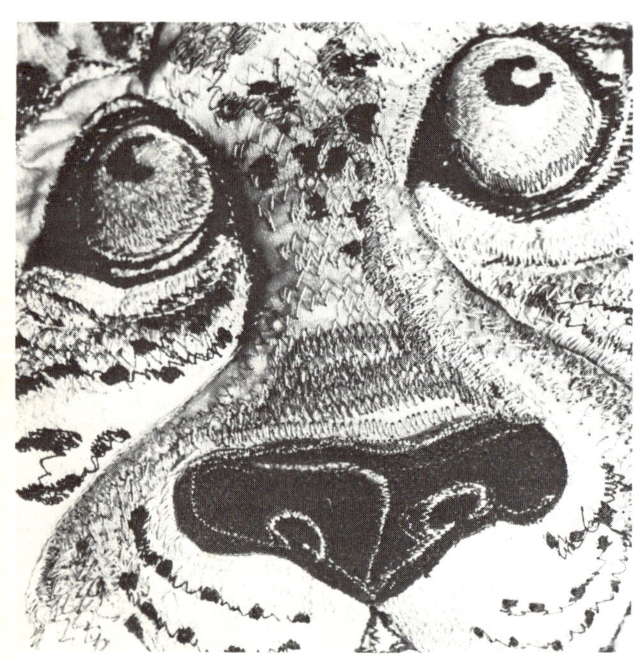

130. *Detail of the Leopard Poncho showing the satin stitching, blobs, and free-machined quilting on the head.*

The caftan is made of unbleached muslin, which I batiked before embroidering. The embroidery here is all free machined, predominately straight stitch, satin stitch, and whip stitch. A detail of the springtime tree (figure C8) shows the closely worked circles of whip stitch like those you did in Lesson 4, suggestive of the soft, featherlike quality of early spring. This stitch creates a lighter, less harshly defined edge and works beautifully for such things as apple blossoms, sheep's wool, and soft summer clouds. The rough texture of the tree bark (figure 128) is done by using the double needle to create a raised line similar to the one you made on the checked gingham in your wall panel (page 51), but this one is done without the presser foot, using the free machining technique. The stiff grey-and-white spines of the hedgehog are stitched with both black and white thread through the same needle (a size 90 needle will allow two threads to go through easily).

This caftan is unusual because the greater part of it is worked with some sort of embroidery. This made it even more important that the caftan be planned as an entire composition—a composition that could be changed but not weakened by movement and distortion when the garment was worn. To accomplish this, I used large, simply-stitched areas such as leaves, blossoms, and branches at the top of the garment, and the patterns of tree roots at the bottom. Areas of repetitive texture—leaves, blossoms, and roots —can be distorted as the garment moves, but the viewer can still understand the design. Focal points were provided by the very personal rendering of animals, plants, and birds. The caftan tells a story, creates a mood and atmosphere, and is a comfortable and delightful garment to wear.

The Poncho

Another version of the simple square-cut garment is the poncho, in this case the "triangular" poncho (figure 129). Here two rectangles of fabric are overlapped and seamed at both ends; it appears triangular only when worn (figure C16). My Leopard Poncho is a tongue-in-cheek wrap, one that makes people uncertain whether to laugh at me or with me. I love cats, but am allergic to them, and this is my way of cuddling one without sneezing. The body of the poncho (and of the leopard) is cut from leopard-print velveteen; it slings around the shoulders, developing into slightly padded and quilted legs and a tail that tucks under the cat's chin. The pads of the feet are applied suedecloth. The head is like a small cushion, made separately, stuffed and quilted, and applied to the garment (figure C15). The face was built up of layers of different fabrics, padded in places, quilted, and appliquéd like your apple project in exercise 23, page 47. The entire garment is lined.

The Needle-lace Caftan

Figure C17 shows a detail of a square-cut caftan that features needle-lace techniques (page 69). The fabric is very loosely woven (the kind used in the shag bag), with vertical stripes of blue thread running through the natural-colored linen. These threads were gently pulled up from the bottom to the bustline; at the bustline they were pinned in clusters on the surface, then couched down and worked into the needle lace. The needle lace was worked above the bustline, from side to side, forming a continuous sleeve/yoke area. Blue and natural-colored threads were used in the stitching, and the clustered blue threads were knotted and worked into the texture of the piece along with several kinds of beads. The suggestion of a necklace was made of wrapped cords (see page 71) that were shaped into an asymmetrical arabesqué pattern, applied around the neck, and allowed to hang free below the yoke as a pendant. The free-hanging part, which bears an unglazed clay medallion, is fastened to the yoke with Velcro and can be easily removed.

This last project is probably not one you'd like to try immediately as it involves more complicated procedures than the wall hanging or totes did. But can you envision this same caftan with the sleeve/yoke area done in hit-and-miss patchwork or a striking, bold design of appliqué? The garment would then suggest a T shape, which leads us to

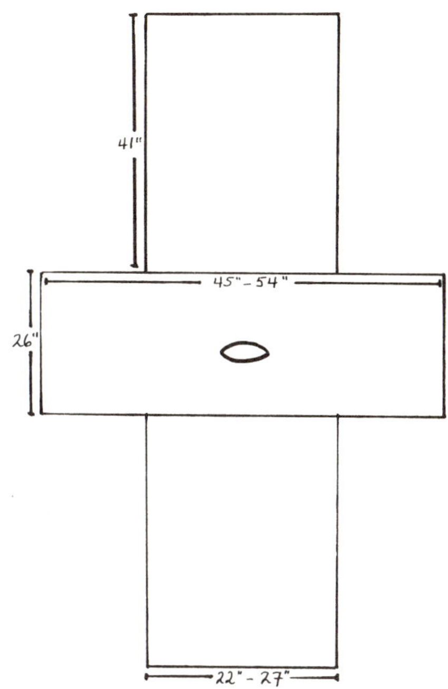

131. Variation of the T cut. The rectangle is the sleeve/yoke piece; the appendages become the front and back of the caftan.

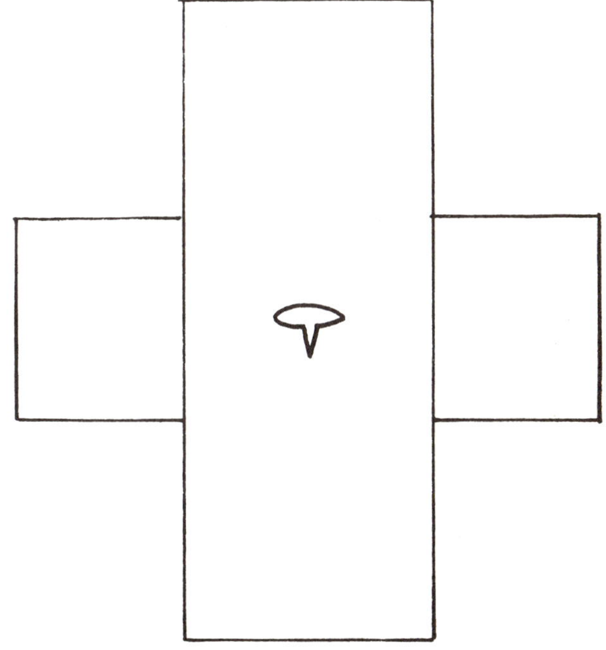

132. Another variation of the T cut. The body of the caftan is the rectangle; the sleeves are appendages.

the second type of square-cut garment, the rectangle with appendages that form the front and back (figure 131). This style can also be worked as shown in figure 132, using one continuous piece of fabric from hem to hem, with a neck opening, like the first simple rectangle, but with additional rectangles appended to form sleeves. All kinds of embroidery, as well as variations on the patchwork or appliqué idea, might be used with either style.

The Afghanistan nomad dress (figure C1) is a more complex version of the T cut. Its sleeve/yoke area forms one continuous line from which the rest of the dress hangs, but because of the additional pieces involved I classify it as a composite rectangle (figure 133). The originals of this garment were designed to be worn when riding camels, and they involved a fantastic profusion of colors, patterns, and fabrics—velvets, calicos, satins, cottons: plain, printed, or striped—all worked into a delightful and dramatic patchwork. Beads, coins, and other ornaments were also worked into the piece. A wonderful example that I once saw seemed to have a complicated design worked in some kind of small silver bits; upon closer examination the silver proved to be rows of metal snaps, tops and bottoms, stitched side by side to form an extremely intricate and decorative pattern!

The front of this dress is gathered and stitched to the basic sleeve/yoke piece, as is the tiered and gathered back. The dress shown here began with an antique embroidered yoke. I added related, free-machined embroidery (figure C2) to the remainder of the dress, using patchwork (some hit-and-miss, some a bit more calculated), applied braids, rickrack, ribbons, and striped fabric altered and enriched with rows of automatic cam stitching. This eye-catching dress presents an exciting problem of color and value distribution—one in which color and pattern ran riot.

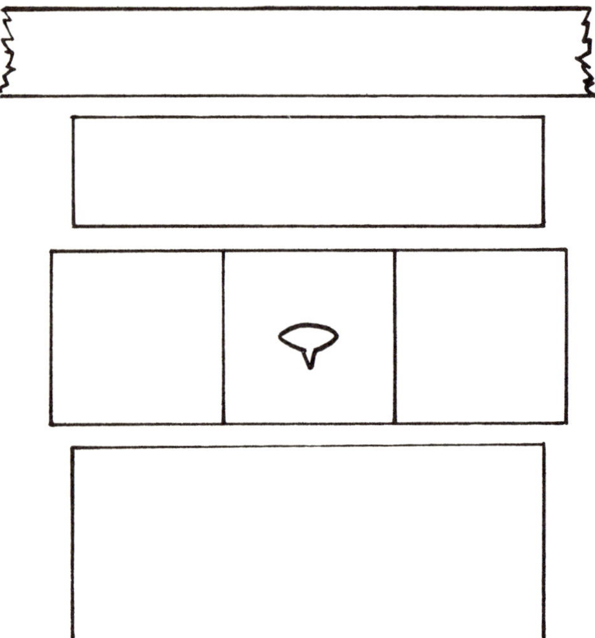

133. Pattern for the tiered Afghanistan nomad dress: a composite rectangle.

Small Treasures

So far, most of the exercises and projects suggested in this book have been on a fairly large scale, in keeping with the freedom and mobility of machine embroidery. It is also easier for the beginning embroiderer to work on a medium- to large-scale project than to try to focus on a small, more detailed piece. But one of the joys of machining is that it is so ideally suited to the precious, small-scale type of embroidery. This fineness of detail can be achieved only by machining, hence when I wanted a tiny piece of crewel for my daughter's dollhouse embroidery frame (scale 1 inch to 1 foot), I turned to the machine.

PENDANTS

Basic Pendant

Work for a dollhouse is detail in the extreme. A more reasonable small piece might be the cat pendant (figure 135). It measures 4 inches by 3 inches and is extremely easy to construct. Any simple, stylized design would be effective used in this way: a shell, a snail, a leaf, a fish, or even one of the apples from your sampler. Use an 8-inch hoop for a piece this size. My cat has yellow eyes and is worked in black-and-brown satin stitch at a setting from 1 to 4 in width, on natural-colored linen. A second piece of linen the same size and shape is used for the back. Place the two pieces, right sides together, and seam like a pillow cover, allowing a

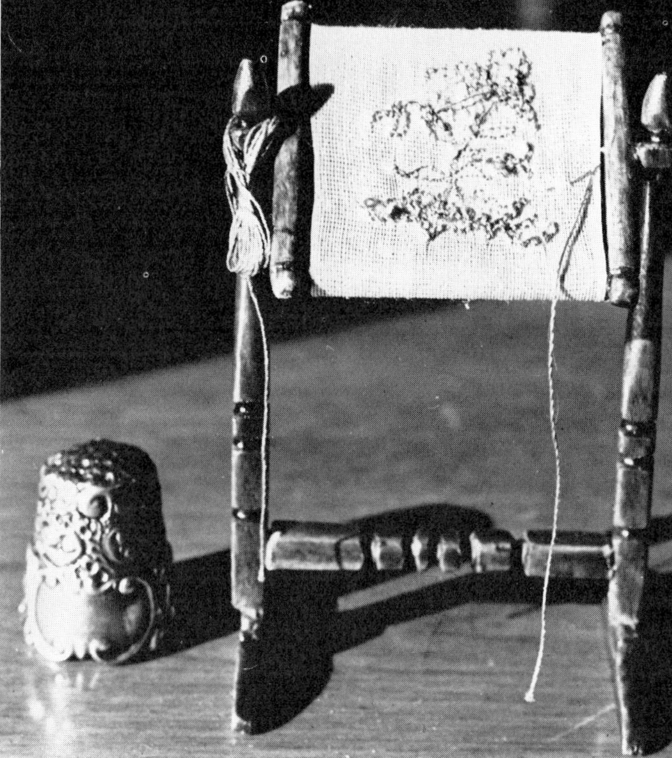

134. *Miniature embroidery frame scaled an inch to a foot, with a thimble at the side to show size. The "crewel" was worked on the machine; the "yarn" is ordinary thread.*

135. *A simple, stylized cat design used for a pendant.*

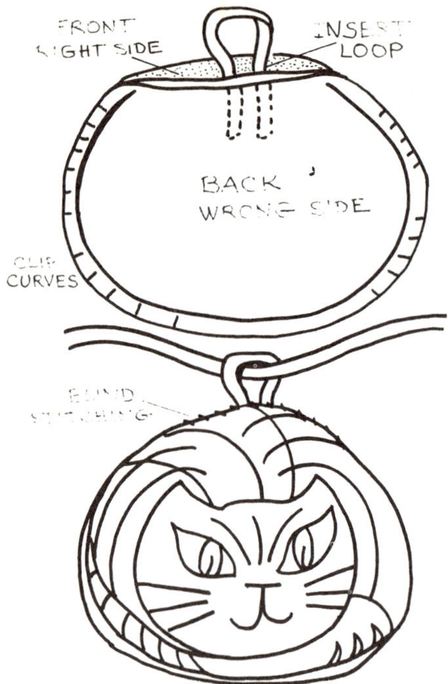

136. Construction of the cat pendant.

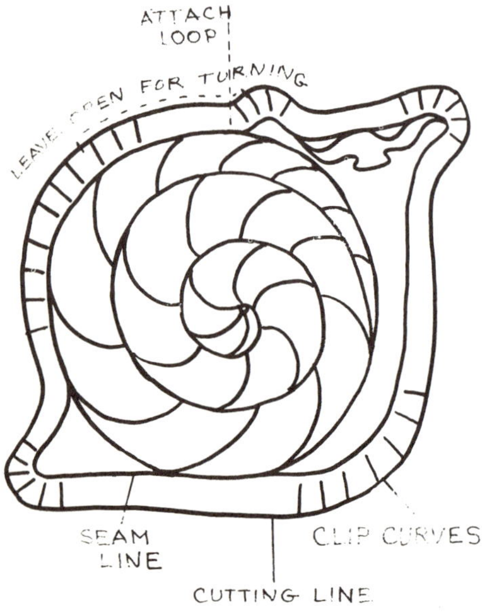

137. Pattern for quilted snail pendant.

3-inch opening at the top for turning. After turning and pressing, insert a loop of yarn, a metal or plastic ring, or a loop of leather in the opening, before blind stitching it closed. Press again and the pendant is ready to be hung from a chain, cord, or leather thong.

Padded Pendant

If lightweight fabric is used for a pendant, I'd recommend a Pellon or muslin interlining to add body. This project, incidentally, is ideal for padding or stuffing. The convolutions of a snail shell would lend themselves well to this sort of treatment. For such a project, use a fairly lightweight top fabric and an unbleached muslin interlining. Transfer the design to the top fabric with a transfer pencil, a paper pattern (see page 80), or chalk. Frame up the top and the interlining and embroider your design, delineating the contours of the shell with free-machined straight stitching. To stuff the snail proceed as follows: remove the fabric sandwich from the hoop, then, working from the back, make a small slit in the muslin interfacing in each section where padding is desired (see figure 138); poke small bits of polyfill into these areas, padding them just enough to raise contours on the front. When the stuffing is completed, close each slit with hand-worked herringbone stitches (figure 139), and finish with a piece of backing fabric and a loop as described for the cat pendant. This form of padding/stuffing is called *trapunto*.

Textured Pendant

An abstract, highly textured pendant could be made using the needle-lace technique described on page 69. For this, work a small piece of needle lace, allowing the withdrawn threads to dangle at the bottom; other types of threads could be added as well as knots and small beads, similar to the fringe on the shag bag (figure 105). This pendant needs no backing since part of its charm is the pattern of openwork. However, it can be backed with a contrasting colored fabric, perhaps picking up a color in the added threads and beads. To back this piece, pin the pendant on the backing fabric (cut larger than size), wrong sides facing. Frame the pendant and backing in a hoop, and free machine in satin stitch around the top and sides of the piece, at the same time working in a loop for hanging. Cut away the excess backing fabric, then stitch a second row of satin stitch on the three edges, this time using either free machining and the quilting foot (no hoop), or teeth and the embroidery foot without the hoop. This should make a neatly stitched, firm edge. To finish the bottom, lift the dangling threads and, using No. 4 zigzag, finish the raw edge of the backing. This can then be lightly stitched at intervals to the dangling threads, or simply left to hang free.

These little pendants are an unusual, eye-catching type of jewelry that packs and travels easily, never needs a lock box, and, better still, is fun to make!

BOXES

Containers have an eternal appeal, not only aesthetically but emotionally. From the moment when early man first pried open an oyster shell and found a pearl, to the time when a Russian czar opened a Fabergé Easter egg, containers and their contents have delighted the world. And closely allied with this pleasure is the joy of creating a container with a surprise or a story. Each of the small boxes I've made either suggests a story or contains a surprise. A Noah's Ark Box shows the procession of animals to the ark, which is stitched on the top; on the inside of the lid is the dove surrounded by a circular rainbow, and inside the box itself a cheerful little flower springs up from a hillock of dry land—the promise of hope and renewal. Then there are more—a Cat and Mouse Box (figure C20), a Bog Box, a Daytime Cat-Nighttime Cat Box, and a Strawberry Surprise— all made from a few threads, some fabric, and tuna-fish cans. All are splendidly scaled to the delicacy and maneuverability of machine embroidery.

Not all boxes need to be petite, however. A shortening tin,

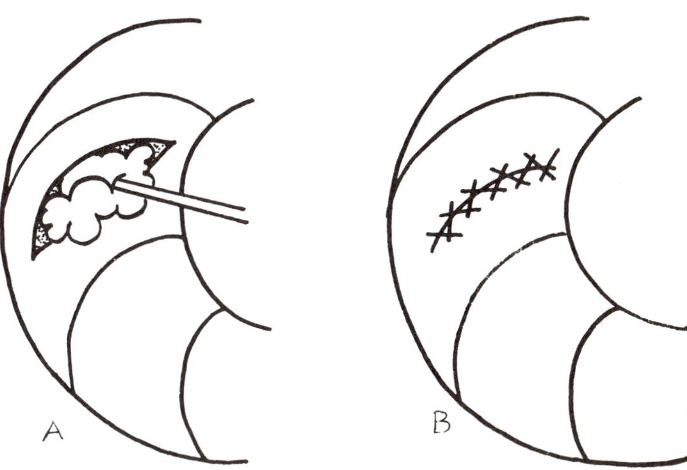

138. *Trapunto. A. Stuffing inserted into slit in back of snail. B. Slit closed with hand-worked herringbone stitching.*

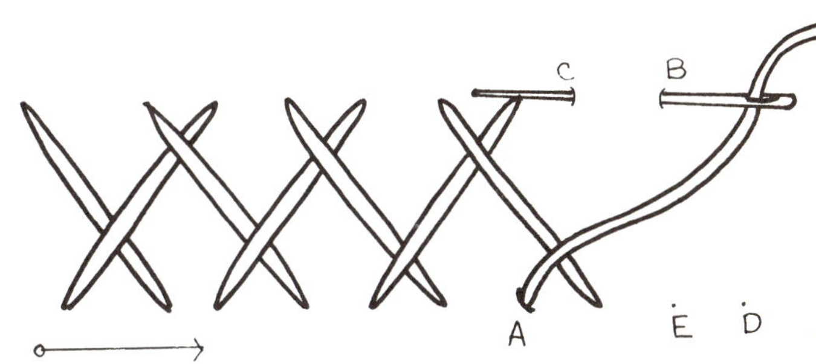

139. *Herringbone stitch. Work from left to right.*

140. The Cat and Mouse Box, made from a tuna-fish can, features on its lid a soft-sculptured cat made of nylon hose and stuffed with polyfill. The body of the box is satin stitching, whip stitching, and blobs on printed fabric. The tiny ball of yarn is part of the fastening.

141. Detail of the Elemental Box showing three seasons. Spring furrows, left, are stitched with a double needle. Spring fades into fully leafed summer trees, cable stitched with heavy perle cotton in the bobbin, and summer changes to the fallen leaves of autumn.

a coffee can, or any other kind of can will provide room for an even greater flight of fancy. The Elemental Box (figures on these pages and C5, C18, and C19) was made from a four-pound tuna-fish can and is 5 inches high, 6 inches in diameter. Its theme is based on the classical concept of the four elements of the universe: earth, air, fire, and water. The outside, earth, shows the four seasons. The outside lid, air, shows a quiet summer sky highlighted by a puffy, free-quilted cloud; the inside lid shows a starry nighttime sky. The inner sides of the box are appliquéd with flamelike shapes in red velvet; tongues of green net enrich the reds and suggest hazy smoke rising from the fire. Finally, the inside bottom of the box, water, suggests the underwater life of the sea.

As you can see, part of the fun in embroidering a box is choosing a theme. Think of one that suggests a story or some kind of surprise: "In the beginning . . . ," the Pied Piper, Pandora revisited, Fingal's cave—all suggest possibilities to me. You'll have many other ideas, I'm sure.

The amount of fabric required for the smallest-size tuna-fish can is minimal: 12 inches by 25 inches for the outside top, sides, and bottom. A lightweight, slightly stretchy fabric is best, especially for the outside. The same size will do the inside wall, top, and bottom. A lightweight fabric is important for the inside, since unnecessary bulk would be a problem. Nets, sheers, and nylon hose are useful, and a small amount of dacron polyfill for quilting, stuffing, and padding is necessary, and of course you'll need your usual range of threads for machining. In addition you will need some lightweight corrugated cardboard (grocery-store carton variety), pins, and white glue. And an empty seven-ounce tuna-fish can, lid removed, bottom left in.

Since the size involved is so small, it will be easy to plan your design as a complete composition, relating one area and idea to another. And as you plan your design, think of your broadening knowledge of machine-embroidery techniques and try to use it in new and exciting ways. Think too of a type of closure for your box, if indeed it needs one. My Cat and Mouse Box has a soft-sculptured cat asleep on top (the mouse is very wide awake inside), and a ball of yarn dangles from the cat's paw. The ball of yarn serves as a knob around which a length of yarn loops to form a closure for the box. The Bog Box has a small stone on top around which a loop of elastic thread can be fastened, making a closing that also blends in with the weeds and cattails around the sides. My Elemental Box (figure 141) requires no closure. Either way, decide in advance about the mechanics of a fastening, and plan for it as part of your composition.

Constructing a Box

Read the following instructions all the way through before you start making a box; that way you'll know how your embroidery will be attached to the can. Once you've done your stitching, lightly fluff the embroidery with a steam iron if the finished pieces require it, but do not flatten the stitching.

Sides

Mark the midpoint of the embroidered strips that will cover the inner and outer sides of the box. Right sides together, pin the outer side to the inner side along what will be the top edge of the box, starting from the center and slightly stretching the outer side while slightly compacting the inner side. (The outer surface of the box is slightly larger in circumference than the inner, hence this easing.) Using a normal dressmaking setting, stitch this seam; press the seam to the inner side and trim to 3/8 inch. Trim any excess fabric to 1½ inches at the inside bottom and the outside bottom, 3/8 inch at the point where your side seam will be.

With the wrong side out, fit the outer side to the can, allowing the inner side to project above the rim of the can, and fit the outer side snugly without stretching the fabric. Mark the seam line. Right sides together, machine stitch this seam, making the inner side seam ½-inch deeper (that is, making the inner piece a bit smaller than the outer one, thus providing a snugger fit—figure 145). Press the seam

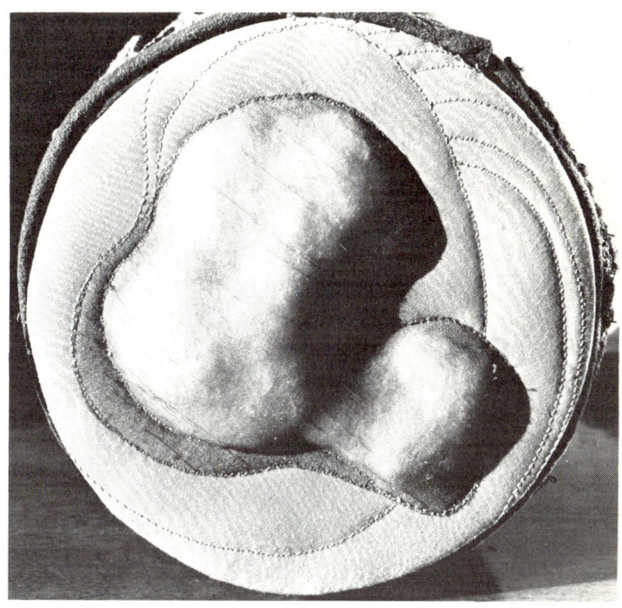

142. *Daytime sky on the outside top of the Elemental Box. Dacron polyfill provides dimension to a free-form, free-quilted cloud.*

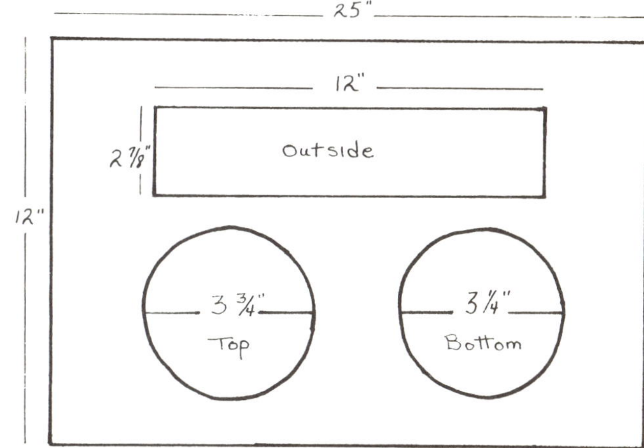

143. *Pattern for fabric that will cover the outside of an embroidered box. It is best to embroider slightly outside these dimensions for flexibility in fitting to the can. Extra fabric is for seams and framing in the hoop. Slightly smaller dimensions are required for inside areas. Fit the embroidered pieces to the can before trimming away excess fabric.*

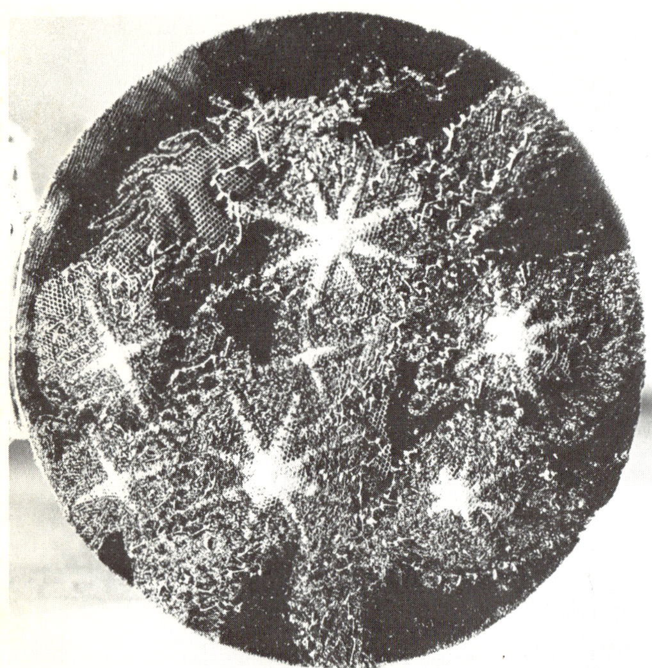

144. *Inside lid of Elemental Box showing the nighttime sky. Yellow and gold metallic stars are stitched over black velvet covered with layers of black net and blue net. Whip stitch (black thread on top, blue, yellow, and red threads in the bobbin) suggests distant galaxies.*

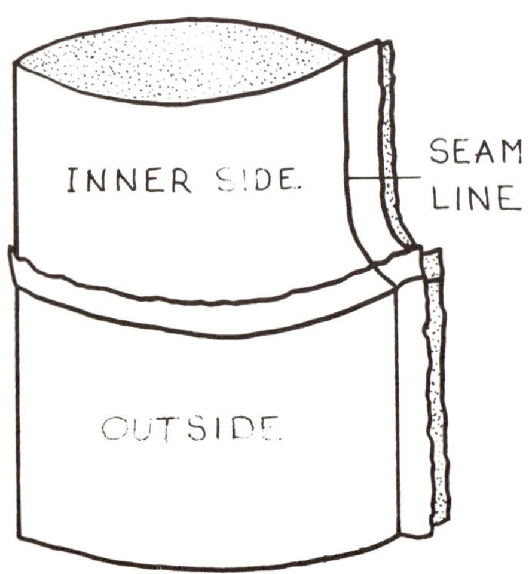

145. *Covering for the sides of the box, stitched together and shown from the wrong side.*

open and flat, and turn the fabric to the right side. At this point the front closure should be attached to the seam so the closure can be worked into the design as an organic part of the piece. The seam itself may be disguised with embroidery or appliqué.

Glue a thin layer of polyfill around the outside of the can and cover with a layer of nylon hose glued to the outside bottom, stretched taut up over the top, and extending to the inside of the can. Fit the nylon smoothly on the inside by cutting away excess folds and then secure it neatly with glue. Allow to dry. (The reason for the nylon is that fabric can be slid over it easily and that it prevents the polyfill from shifting.)

Carefully slide the outer side of your embroidered fabric over the can, easing it into place over the padding. The top seam should be at the upper rim, the seam allowance inside the can, and the side seam at what will be the front. The inner side fabric stands up above the rim of the can. (The side seam is at the front of the can because this is the easiest place to hide the seam, since you may be making a closure. This location also means that when you open the box, the seam will not be the first thing you see.)

With heavy thread doubled through a large needle, gather by hand the lower edge of the outer fabric ½ inch from the bottom edge; pull the gathers tight (like a mob cap) and lash the gathers securely into place across the bottom with the gathering thread. Make sure the outer side is taut but has no undue stretching.

Top

Cut a cardboard circle ¼ inch larger in diameter than the top of the can. Pad it slightly as for the can side if you wish. Cut your embroidered top piece 1½ inches larger than the cardboard, gather the surplus material as you did for the bottom, and lace into place, fitting the fabric snugly but not distorting the cardboard. Additional or alternate closure details can be added at this time. Trim the fabric for the inner lid ½ inch larger than the cardboard; turn under the edges and carefully pin into position on the inner lid. Blind stitch the fabric in place by hand.

Inside Bottom

Cut a cardboard circle to fit *snugly* inside the can. Remember, the fabric will create some bulk so fit this circle very carefully. Cover the inner bottom as you did the outer top (usually no padding is necessary here unless your particular theme requires it). Set the inner bottom aside. Touch a bit of glue to the lower inside of the can and smooth the inner side fabric carefully into place, making it taut but not distorted. Distribute the excess fabric evenly around the bottom of the can, and cut away any untidy bulk. You will probably not need to gather the excess with thread, but do so if you wish. Carefully place a small amount of glue around the bottom/side juncture and on the bottom of the can. Now, with one solid, downward motion force the covered bottom firmly into the bottom of the can and weight it until the glue is dry. This should firm up the side fabric, and create a well-upholstered interior.

Lid

Position the top carefully on the box, noting alignment in both open and closed positions; from inside, hand stitch the lid to the can with three or four small herringbone stitches worked one on top of the other to form a small hinge (see herringbone diagram, page 89).

Outside Bottom

Although you'll probably have no embroidery on the fabric you're using for the bottom of your box, you might want to stitch on your signature. Cut a cardboard circle a shade smaller than the bottom of the can and cover the cardboard with fabric—signed or not—as for the inside bottom. No padding is necessary. Glue in place and secure with five or six evenly spaced rubber bands until the glue is dry.

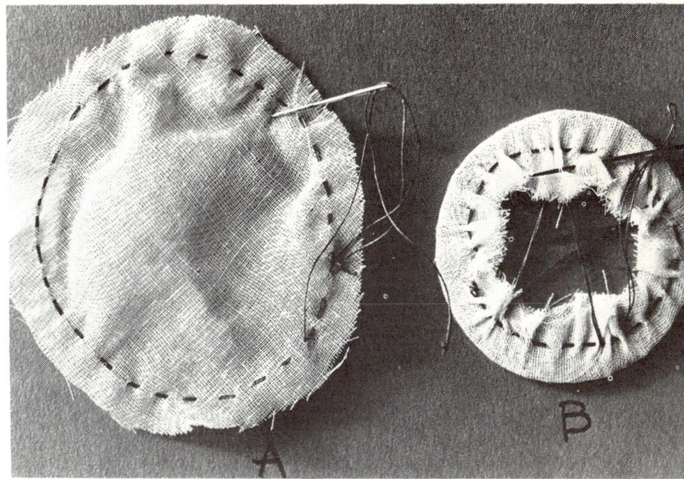

146. *Construction of the box top and bottom. A. The circle of fabric is gathered by hand with strong running stitches. B. Fabric is fitted over a cardboard circle and the stitches are gathered tightly and lashed into place.*

147. *Detail of the Elemental Box showing autumn fading into winter. Fallen leaves (left) are suggested by stitching over layers of vegetable-bag mesh, net, and nylon hose. See also figure C18.*

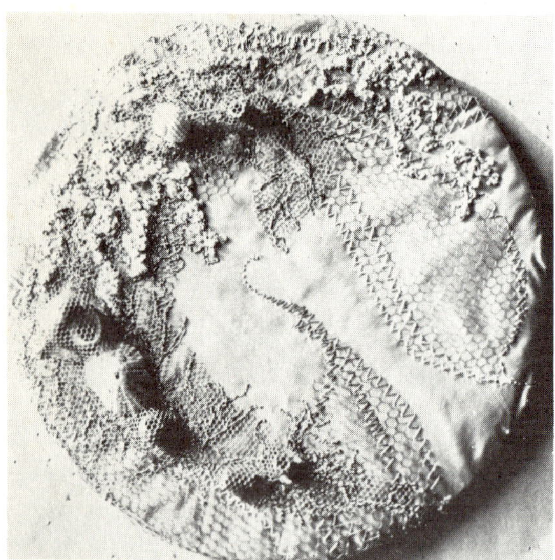

148. *Bottom inside of Elemental Box showing water. Clumps of beads and shells arranged over blue-green chintz are held in place with net.*

These boxes were developed during six months when my husband and I shared one small dormitory room in London: lack of space dictated that my embroidery projects be small. But by now I'm sure you've discovered that size of project does not limit the scope of a machine embroiderer's world.

The true joy of your new art will come when you feel free to express your ideas without having to concentrate on techniques: when you develop new sensitivity to relationships of line, area, and color, and when you look at the world through an embroiderer's eyes. Your new skill in machine embroidery, combined with your stimulated imagination, can show you a new and exciting world: from apples to appliqué, from cats to couching, from tuna-fish cans to treasures.

Those of us who embroider are indeed privileged. I know of no other art form that has remained so closely allied with the rich treasures of its past while offering unlimited opportunity for contemporary, personal fulfillment.

> Love, when you sew, your needle's point advanceth
> And makes it dance a thousand curious strains
> Of winding rounds, whereof the form remains,
> To show that your fair hands can dance the hey,
> Which your fine feet would learn as well as they.
> —Sir John Davies, *Orchestra*, 1596

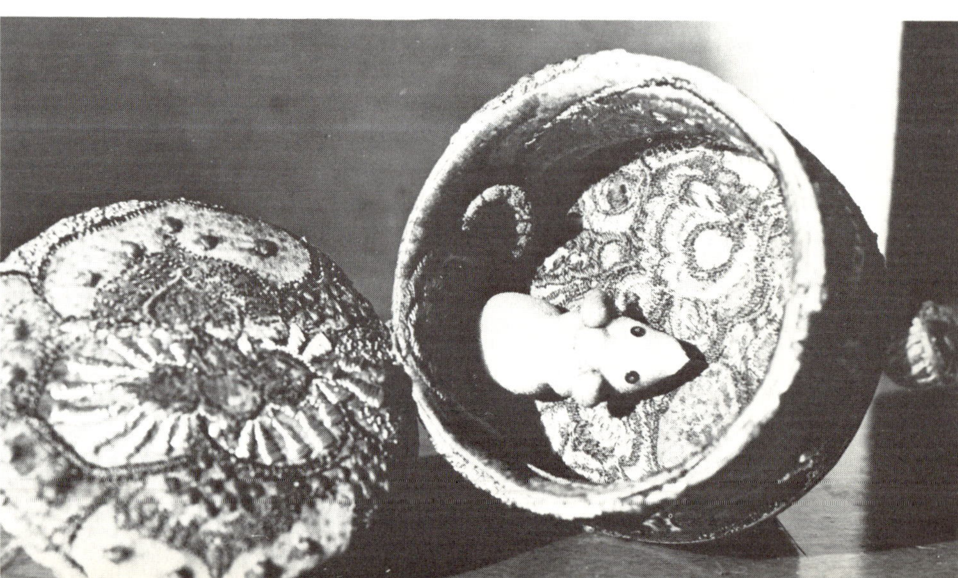

149. *Interior of Cat and Mouse Box.*

BIBLIOGRAPHY

Bartley, Regina. *The Joy of Machine Embroidery.* Chicago: Henry Regnery, 1976.

Butler, Anne. *Machine Stitches.* London: Batsford, 1976.

Clucas, Joy. *Your Machine for Embroidery.* London: G. Bell & Sons, 1973.

Fanning, Robbie. *Decorative Machine Stitchery.* New York: Butterick, 1976.

Gray, Jennifer. *Machine Embroidery.* New York: Van Nostrand Reinhold, 1973.

Hall, Carolyn V. *The Sewing Machine Craft Book.* New York: Van Nostrand Reinhold, 1980.

Nicholas, Annwen and Daphne Teague. *Embroidery in Fashion.* London: Pitman, 1975.

Risley, Christine. *Machine Embroidery.* London: Studio Vista, 1973.

Singer Instructions for Art Embroidery. New York: Singer Sewing Machine Company in America, 1911.

Swift, Gay. *Machine Stitchery.* Newton Center, Massachusetts: Charles T. Branford Company, 1974.

GLOSSARY

Achromatic color scheme: the scheme formed by using only black, white, and their tints and shades; a scheme without color.

Achromatic neutral: any grey formed by mixing only black and white.

Analogous (adjacent) color scheme: the scheme formed by using several hues, plus their tints and shades, that lie side by side on the color wheel; the scheme should include only one dominant primary color.

Appliqué: the technique of stitching a shape cut from one fabric to the surface of another fabric.

Area: the space bounded by a line, actual or implied.

Bargello pattern: a type of canvas embroidery worked in Gobelin stitch, probably taking its name from an ancient fortress, now a museum, in Florence.

Batik: a cold-water, wax-resist dyeing process. When the fabric is dyed, the color of the fabric is retained in areas that have been painted in wax. Additional dyeing and waxing can add new colors and design elements.

Bella Donna: a shiny, twisted, rayon thread.

Blind hemming stitch: an automatic cam setting that straight stitches for three or four stitches, then zigzags for one stitch.

Blob: a heavy build-up of thread in one spot, formed by using the zigzag stitch without moving the fabric.

Cable stitch: a machine stitch worked from the wrong side of the fabric in which the bobbin thread becomes the top thread; the technique allows the embroiderer to use heavy threads that cannot pass through the eye of the needle.

Caftan: a traditional Mid-Eastern floor-length garment, rectangular in shape, with sleeves and a hood; in the popular sense, a simple, square-cut garment that is seamed at the sides and has an opening for the neck.

Cam stitches: automatic pattern stitches available on some sewing machines.

Chromatic neutral: any grey formed by mixing black, white, and a small amount of a color.

Collage: here a composition made of small bits and pieces of fabrics, threads, beads, and other odds and ends, all stitched into a unified whole. *Collage* comes from *coller, to paste* in French.

Complementary color scheme: a scheme formed by using those hues, plus their tints and shades, that are directly opposite each other on the color wheel.

Couching: the process of fastening one thread down with another so that only the second thread passes through the fabric.

Darning foot: see quilting foot.

Double needle: a needle that stitches two lines simultaneously. This needle varies with the type and age of the machine: one type is in fact two needles, the other is a lyre-shaped needle with a single shank and two points. Triple needles are also available for some machines.

Drawn fabric: openwork embroidery in which fabric threads are moved and distorted with stitches to create a pattern. Not to be confused with *drawn-thread work,* another type of openwork embroidery. In drawn-thread work, the pattern is created when some fabric threads are withdrawn and others are clumped together with stitches. Both processes are used in needle lace.

Dressmaking setting: a setting that uses the teeth, the presser foot, normal tension top and bottom, stitch width of 0, stitch length of 2 (on a scale of 4), and no hoop.

Encroaching satin stitch: closely spaced zigzag stitches that interlock, forming an overall unpatterned texture.

Examplar or sampler: fabric with stitches worked on it to demonstrate an embroiderer's vocabulary; in effect, a stitchery "textbook" that, from the fifteenth century onward, was passed from one generation to the next.

Florentine pattern: a pattern of Gobelin stitches worked on canvas, probably named for the area around Florence. Many variations of this pattern are recognized.

Free-machine quilting: free machining worked on two layers of fabric with a layer of padding in between; it both stitches the layers of fabric together, and creates a design with the stitching. Worked with a quilting (darning) foot, with or without a hoop.

Free-machine satin stitch: closely spaced zigzag stitches worked with the free machine setting.

Free machine setting: a setting that uses dropped or covered teeth, normal tension top and bottom, variable stitch width, and no presser foot. Stitch length is of no consequence; fabric is usually framed in a hoop.

Free machining: machine embroidery usually worked in a hoop, with the presser foot removed and teeth covered or dropped. The fabric is free to move easily in all directions.

Gobelin stitch: a satin stitch worked on "needlepoint" canvas.

Hard edge: strong, distinct contrast between positive and negative areas.

Hit-and-miss patchwork: random patchwork formed from strips of fabric pieces that have been seamed together, cut, turned, and reseamed, with the process repeated until a patchwork fabric is created.

Hue: a specific color: red, green, or blue, for example.

Knot (machined): a tiny build-up of thread in one spot that forms a subtle, knotlike texture; formed by using the straight stitch without moving the fabric.

Line: that which connects two points.

Machine satin stitch: a line of closely spaced zigzag stitching using a variable stitch width (1 to 4 on a scale of 1 to 4) and a stitch length of ½ on a scale of 1 to 4.

Monochromatic color scheme: a scheme using only one hue plus its tints and shades.

Needle lace: an openwork pattern created by clumping the threads from loosely woven fabric with the zigzag stitch; sometimes threads are withdrawn from the fabric before the fabric is stitched.

Negative area: an unstitched area; the area of a composition that appears to recede.

Persian wool: a popular three-ply, twisted, all-purpose wool thread.

Pin tucking: rows of tiny tucks; in machining, subtle ridges formed by stitching with the double needle.

Poncho: a short, square-cut ethnic garment; often simply an unseamed rectangle of fabric with a hole for the neck.

Positive area: a stitched area; the dominant area of a composition.

Powdering (seeding): the technique of filling an area with small, individual stitches or motifs.

Presser foot: the stabilizing foot that rides on the surface of the fabric and surrounds the needle where it pierces the fabric.

Presser-foot bar: the lever, usually at the back of the machine, that raises and lowers the presser foot.

Primary color: one of three basic prismatic hues from which other colors can be mixed—red, yellow, and blue.

Quilting (darning) foot: an accessory foot with a spring shank; it stabilizes the surface of the fabric yet allows the fabric to be moved easily for free machining.

Satin stitch: closely spaced parallel stitches that create a smooth embroidered surface.

Scumbling: filling an area with widely spaced, free-machined zigzag, much like a painter's use of a thin turpentine wash to indicate color, value, and form.

Secondary color: a hue formed by mixing one primary with another primary. Green, orange, and violet are examples of secondary colors.

Seeding: see powdering.

Shade: a dark value of a color.

Soft edge: an indistinct, gentle contrast between positive and negative areas.

Sole plate: the metal plate on the surface of a sewing machine that contains a small opening through which the needle passes to engage with the bobbin thread underneath.

Spiderweb: a web-shaped design made by working machine stitching over an opening cut in the fabric.

Split complementary color scheme: a scheme formed by using a hue and two other hues. The second two are on either side of the direct complement of the first.

Square-cut garment: a simple garment made of square or rectangular pieces of fabric, constructed without shaping or fitting devices such as darts, tucks, or pleats; often a traditional ethnic style.

Stitch Witchery: a commercial bonding agent applied with a warm iron, available in fabric and notions shops.

Swing-needle machine: zigzag sewing machine.

Tertiary color: a hue formed by mixing together one primary and one secondary color.

Texture: the feel of a surface—rough, smooth, soft, hard, shiny, dull.

Tint: a light value of a color.

Tone: a hue to which another color or grey has been added, resulting in a softened or greyed effect.

Transfer pencil: a soft, waxy pencil that makes a mark that can be transferred from paper to fabric with a warm iron.

Trapunto: a form of quilting that raises selected areas. Two pieces of fabric are stitched together, then selected areas of the underside fabric are either slit or fabric threads are separated enough to allow stuffing to be inserted. After stuffing, the separated threads are pushed back into place or the slit is closed with stitching.

Value: the lightness or darkness of a color.

Volume: actual or implied depth or third dimension.

Waled satin stitch: closely spaced lines of zigzag arranged side by side to fill an area, creating a waled or cordlike texture.

Welting: flexible cord covered with a strip of bias-cut fabric and set into a seam; used as a finishing edge for cushions, bags, and garments.

Whip stitch: a machine stitch formed when the top tension is tighter than the bottom tension, causing the bottom thread to be pulled up and whipped around the top thread.